2014
FIFA World Cup
Brazil™

OFFICIAL BOOK

This edition published in 2014

Copyright © Carlton Books Limited 2014

Carlton Books Limited
20 Mortimer Street
London W1T 3JW

A CIP catalogue record for this book is available from the British Library

10 9 8 7 6 5 4 3 2 1

ISBN: 978-1-78097-470-5

Project Art Editor: Darren Jordan
Book designer: Mark Tattersall
Editorial: Andrew McDermott
Picture research: Paul Langan
Production: Rachel Burgess
Project Director: Martin Corteel

Manufactured under licence by
Carlton Books Limited

Printed in Italy

2014
FIFA World Cup
Brazil™

OFFICIAL BOOK

CONTENTS

FIFA WORLD CUP
Brasil

INTRODUCTION

FIFA WORLD CUP
Brasil

Brazil has produced some of the greatest players and most iconic moments in the history of the FIFA World Cup. Now, for the first time in 64 years, the spiritual home of football will provide a fitting backdrop for the latest edition of the sport's showpiece event.

A culturally diverse country renowned for its abundance of colour, flavour, sounds and customs is the ideal venue as 32 teams from around the globe come together in South America to showcase their talent.

No country has enjoyed more success on a global stage than Brazil. Ever since a teenage Pele inspired them to victory in 1958, they have been the dominant team with five tournament wins across four different continents.

They also hold the distinction of being the only country to have played in all 19 previous editions of the tournament and their presence at the 2014 finals was guaranteed in October 2007 when they were officially confirmed as hosts for the second time.

Cities across the country's five regions will play host to teams, fans and media from around the world and they are assured of a warm welcome as Brazilians and visitors alike unite "all in one rhythm", to use the words of the official slogan.

Whether it is inside one of the 12 stunning stadiums that have been built or renovated for the finals, or at one of the FIFA Fan Fests in the host cities, being in Brazil during the FIFA World Cup finals will be a unique experience that will live forever in the memory of those who are fortunate enough to be there.

The FIFA Confederations Cup 2013 gave the world a preview of the passion that Brazil's football-crazy fans will bring to the tournament, most notably during the final when the hosts faced reigning world champions Spain at the iconic Maracana. The singing of the national anthem prior to kick-off was an unforgettable demonstration of national pride in front of a global audience.

FIFA President Joseph S. Blatter said: "What we witnessed was something that I have never witnessed. The Maracana has something very exceptional. When I first visited the Maracana in '75, and then years later, there's always something special, that roar. I always said you can compare such a stadium to a church – not a church but a cathedral.

"The fans were extraordinary in the stadium. When they started to sing the national anthem, even when the official part of it was over, they continued to sing. In the final, I would say that history was written in Brazil because the new, remodelled Maracana stadium was given to the national team and they won a big title."

Winning titles is nothing new for Brazil but never before have they won the FIFA World Cup in front of their own fans. Now is the chance for the current squad to write their own place in the history books, but there are 31 teams with other ideas as football prepares to dance to the samba beat.

Above: The Maracana is a cathedral of football, says FIFA President Joseph S. Blatter.

Opposite: Football legend Pele welcomes the world to Brazil as the draw for the 2014 FIFA World Cup is made.

FIFA WORLD CUP
Brasil

The iconic statue of Christ the Redeemer, towering above the Maracana Stadium in Rio de Janeiro, will become a familiar sight during 2014 FIFA World Cup Brazil.

WELCOME TO BRAZIL

Brazilian football fans are among the most passionate on the planet and now, for the first time since 1950, they have the chance to see the world's greatest teams on home soil as the country comes together to host the 2014 FIFA World Cup. The football carnival will be held in 12 stunning venues which will provide a fitting stage for a long-awaited tournament.

THE STAGE IS SET

FIFA WORLD CUP
Brasil

Brazil may have been the sole candidate to host the 2014 FIFA World Cup but in the months leading up to the award of the tournament, the country was left in no doubt that being made hosts was not going to be a foregone conclusion.

Under the continental rotation system that was in operation at the time, it was known that South America would stage the FIFA World Cup in 2014. Initially, Brazil and Colombia had indicated their wish to be considered, but in April 2007 – some six months before the decision was due to be made – Colombia announced it was withdrawing its bid.

That left Brazil as the sole candidate but both the Confederacao Brasileira de Futebol (CBF) and FIFA made it clear that they were taking nothing for granted. FIFA president Joseph S. Blatter pointed out that a final

decision could easily be put off for a year if all the stipulated requirements were not achieved.

Blatter said in April 2007: "For the time being, Brazil has not yet been given the World Cup. If something should happen to the Brazil bid, then we still have time to start again as we are a year in advance of the decision-making process for previous World Cups."

Brazil, which previously hosted the finals back in 1950 and which was aware that there was a significant amount of work to do in terms of modernising and building stadia, did not rest on its laurels either. The CBF submitted a

900-page dossier to FIFA detailing its plans in full with a list of 18 possible venues with a 40,000 capacity or higher.

The next step was a visit by a FIFA inspection team to Brazil in August 2007, and it identified that of the 18 stadiums, four would have to be built from scratch and all of the other 14 undergo substantial renovation.

At that time, many of the stadia were not even equipped for television commentary but FIFA's inspection report stated Brazil was "more than capable of hosting an exceptional FIFA World Cup".

The inspectors said FIFA must maintain close links with the Brazilian organisers – and start immediately. "Brazil has a rich history of hosting sporting and other international events," added the report, "but the standards and demands of the FIFA World Cup will far surpass those of any other event staged in the history of Brazil in terms of magnitude and complexity.

"The inspection team is of the opinion that it would be important for FIFA experts to carefully review the process and progress of host city selection to ensure that adequate financing is committed and secured by the time of the deadline for the selection of the host cities and the related stadium facilities or potential stadium construction sites."

On 30 October 2007, officials from the CBF and Brazil's bidding team gathered at

FIFA headquarters in Zurich for a meeting of the executive committee where it was formally announced that the country would be the 2014 tournament hosts. The announcement sparked celebrations across the country and the FIFA president revealed he had been impressed by Brazil's plans for 2014 despite the fact they were the only bidders.

Blatter said: "The task was not easy – for us it was a real big challenge to have the same list of requirements and the same conditions for only one candidate than if we had two and perhaps we put the bar higher than if we had two. There was an extraordinary presentation by the delegation and we witnessed that this World Cup will have such a big social and cultural impact in Brazil. This is the country that has given to the world the best football and the best footballers, five times world champions. That's why the executive committee has decided unanimously to give the right and the responsibility to organise the 2014 World Cup to Brazil."

After the announcement, Blatter handed the FIFA World Cup Trophy to the then president of Brazil, Luiz Inacio Lula da Silva, who had flown to Zurich for the announcement. Lula responded, saying: "Soccer is not only a sport for us. It's more than that: Soccer for us is a passion, a national passion."

That passion will be there for all to see at the 2014 FIFA World Cup.

Above: FIFA president Joseph S. Blatter (right) and the then Brazilian president, Luiz Inacio Lula da Silva, with the FIFA World Cup Trophy at the announcement in Zurich.

Opposite: Blatter makes the formal announcement after an executive committee meeting at FIFA headquarters in Zurich.

FOOTBALL NATION

FIFA WORLD CUP
Brasil

The names roll off the tongue, conjuring memories of beguiling moments and great deeds in football's world history – Didi, Garrincha, Jairzinho, Tostao, Gerson, Pele, Rivelino, Zico, Socrates, Ronaldo, Rivaldo, Ronaldinho.

They are the Boys from Brazil. Men who have worn the thrilling canary yellow jerseys of Brazil's national team and, in doing so, have become international treasures for football followers who like their sport played with daring and style.

Top of that illustrious list is Edson Arantes do Nascimento, otherwise known as Pele and regarded by many as the greatest footballer who has ever lived.

Not just because he scored 77 goals in 92 appearances for Brazil, or that he is the only footballer to be a member of three World Cup-winning squads, or the fact that he was renowned for his electrifying dribbling and passing, his pace, his powerful shot, his exceptional

heading ability and his prolific goalscoring.

Pele is among the greatest because of the complete package. Because he was as close as it gets to the perfect footballer and as such he encapsulated every facet of Brazil's footballing heritage.

"I was born to play football, just like Beethoven was born to write music," Pele once mused and much the same could be said for so many of the Brazilian greats.

No wonder Brazil is the most successful football nation on earth, having won five FIFA World Cups in 1958, 1962, 1970, 1994 and 2002.

It is also the only national team to have won the World Cup on four different continents. In Europe

(1958 Sweden), in South America (1962 Chile), twice in North America (1970 Mexico and 1994 United States) and once in Asia (2002 Korea/Japan).

It is also the only nation to have played in every World Cup since the tournament was launched in 1930. And the only nation to have kept the trophy, which it did after winning the tournament for the third time in 1970, although the Jules Rimet Trophy, as it was known then, was subsequently stolen in 1983 and thought to have been melted down by thieves.

Yet, for all Garrincha's dribbling and Zico's panache and Pele's brilliance, Brazil's heritage does not come down to individuals. Not really. It comes down to forging great teams with those individuals, none greater than the collection of 1970, renowned as quite probably the greatest team ever to play the world's most popular sport.

That was the team captained by Carlos Alberto, inspired in midfield by Tostao and Rivelino, given penetrating width by Jairzinho and led with sublime grace by Pele.

Who could forget the epic clash in Guadalajara with England, then the reigning world champions, which ended 1–0 to Brazil after arguably the greatest save ever by goalkeeper Gordon Banks from a Pele header, and the famous photograph of Pele and England captain Bobby Moore embracing after the final whistle?

Who could forget Brazil going on to defeat Italy 4–1 with a classic

last goal from Carlos Alberto in a final which celebrated in typically samba fashion the extravagant talents of the world's most gifted footballers?

"The English invented it, the Brazilians perfected it." That is the phrase with which Brazil's fans taunt the rest of the world and there is no doubt that 1970 team set the benchmark for the teams of the future and, while it was 24 years before Brazil lifted the trophy again, the legacy of Pele and Co lives on today.

It is why on 12 June 2014 in Arena de Sao Paulo, when Brazil kick off the 20th FIFA World Cup, the football world expects something extraordinary. Brazil's history suggests they will not disappoint.

Above: Roberto Rivelino, part of the great Brazil team that won the 1970 FIFA World Cup in Mexico.

Right: Pele, arguably the greatest of them all, is chaired off by fans after the 1970 final.

Opposite: Midfield maestro Zico continued the tradition of beautiful Brazilian football.

THE VENUES

FIFA WORLD CUP
Brasil

Brazil is the largest country in South America, covering more than half the continent and, with around 190 million people, is the fifth most populated in the world. The football-crazy country is all set to host the FIFA World Cup for a second time, with games taking place in 12 different cities.

Brazil is one of the most inviting countries on the planet and there are many reasons why it has become such a popular tourist destination. With stunning white sandy beaches, vast rainforests and vibrant cities such as Rio de Janeiro and Sao Paulo, Brazil has so much to offer and these are exciting times for the country as it prepares to host the 2014 FIFA World Cup and then the Olympic and Paralympic Games two years later.

Brazilians are known for their love of a party, with colourful carnivals to rival any in the world. The locals and fans from nations across the globe will strut the samba like never before when the FIFA World Cup is held in Brazil for the first time in 64 years. When the showpiece was first held in the country back in 1950, only six stadiums in as many different cities were used, but the 2014 extravaganza will be a far cry from that tournament.

The biggest stadium and undoubtedly one of the most famous in the world is the Estadio Jornalista Mario Filho, or the Maracana as it is more commonly known. Built for the 1950 FIFA World Cup, the Rio de Janeiro venue has packed in crowds of more than 200,000 and although the capacity will be down to 73,531 for the 2014 FIFA World Cup following major renovation ahead of the tournament, it remains Brazil's biggest stadium.

The Maracana hosted the last match in 1950 (there was no final),

which Brazil lost to Uruguay, and will do so again on 13 July.

As well as Rio de Janeiro, games will be played throughout the country in stadiums both old and new, with the people of Brazil ready to show why they are famous for their hospitality.

Vast amounts of money have been spent on six stadiums constructed specifically for the FIFA World Cup, with five existing venues undergoing refurbishment and the Estadio Mane Garrincha in Brasilia knocked down and replaced by the Estadio Nacional.

One of those new venues is the unique Arena Amazonia in Manaus, a city that is the gateway to

the Amazon rainforest – the largest tropical rainforest on earth. The stadium was designed to resemble a straw basket, a product for which the region is famous, and emphasis was placed on ensuring the venue is environmentally friendly.

Not since 1978 has a FIFA World Cup been held in South America, but Brazil's love of football means it promises to be worth the wait.

Rio de Janeiro's legendary Maracana Stadium, seen here in 2007, will host the final on 13 July 2014.

2014 FIFA World Cup Brazil™

MANAUS 6

FORTALEZA 5

NATAL 7

RECIFE 9

SALVADOR 11

CUIABA 3

BRASILIA 2

BELO HORIZONTE 1

RIO DE JANEIRO 10

SAO PAULO 12

CURITIBA 4

PORTO ALEGRE 8

1 Stadium
North Region
Northeast Region
Centre West Region
Southeast Region
South Region

1	ESTADIO MINEIRAO	5	ESTADIO CASTELAO	9	ARENA PERNAMBUCO
2	ESTADIO NACIONAL	6	ARENA AMAZONIA	10	ESTADIO DO MARACANA
3	ARENA PANTANAL	7	ESTADIO DAS DUNAS	11	ARENA FONTE NOVA
4	ARENA DA BAIXADA	8	ESTADIO BEIRA-RIO	12	ARENA DE SAO PAULO

BELO HORIZONTE

Estadio Mineirao
CITY: Belo Horizonte
CAPACITY: 62,547
MATCHES: Six, including one semi-final

The home to Atletico Mineiro and Cruzeiro is located in the Pampulha neighbourhood in Belo Horizonte and has been redeveloped for the 2014 FIFA World Cup. Fans can enjoy better access to the arena, which retains the vibrant atmosphere that gives it the reputation as one of the best in the world.

BRASILIA

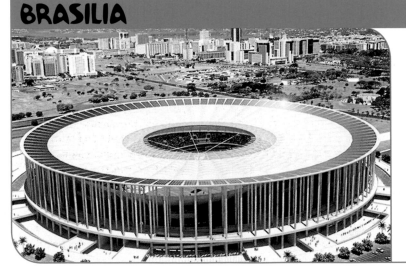

Estadio Nacional
CITY: Brasilia
CAPACITY: 70,042
MATCHES: Seven, including one quarter-final and third-place play-off

Virtually a new venue following the demolition of the existing Estadio Mane Garrincha, the National Stadium is the second largest venue at the FIFA World Cup. The circular facade, with the roof and stands made of metal, is an iconic design and the stadium will be used for concerts and cultural events following the tournament.

CUIABA

Arena Pantanal
CITY: Cuiaba
CAPACITY: 42,968
MATCHES: Four

Pantanal, nicknamed The Big Green because of its construction from sustainable materials, is a purpose-built stadium for the 2014 FIFA World Cup. The design is adaptable, meaning the size is likely to be reduced after the tournament, with local clubs Mixto and Operario set to take up residency.

CURITIBA

Arena da Baixada

CITY: Curitiba
CAPACITY: 41,456
MATCHES: Four

It is fitting that this stadium was chosen as a venue for the 2014 FIFA World Cup as it celebrates its 100th anniversary this year. It has been renovated twice since then, first in 1999 and, most recently, in the build-up to the tournament. Based in the Agua Verde region of Curitiba, it is now a modern arena, the home of Atletico Paranaense.

FORTALEZA

Estadio Castelao

CITY: Fortaleza
CAPACITY: 64,846
MATCHES: Six, including one quarter-final

The Castelao is a majestic stadium, given a new look for the 2014 FIFA World Cup. It will host Brazil in the group stages and Ceara and Fortaleza both play there domestically. It is a modern arena with an underground car park, executive boxes, a VIP area, media centre, mixed zone and fully refurbished dressing rooms.

MANAUS

Arena Amazonia

CITY: Manaus
CAPACITY: 42,374
MATCHES: Four

Tucked away in the far north-west of Brazil, the surrounding area of this revamped stadium will provide as much attraction as the football due to the natural beauty of the Amazon rainforest. The stadium itself is impressive and its design gives a nod to the area's local industry as its shape resembles a straw basket, a product for which the region is famous.

NATAL

Estadio das Dunas
CITY: Natal
CAPACITY: 42,086
MATCHES: Four

This venue is brand new, constructed with the 2014 FIFA World Cup in mind. It was built on the site of the old stadium, known as Machadao, and is now a much more modern and self-sustaining venue. The name relates to the sand dunes that are famous in the Natal region, while the unique wave design also represents the dunes.

PORTO ALEGRE

Estadio Beira-Rio
CITY: Porto Alegre
CAPACITY: 48,849
MATCHES: Five, including one second round

Home to one of Brazil's most famous clubs, Internacional, this venue is nicknamed The Giant of Beira-Rio. The most southerly venue for the 2014 FIFA World Cup, just 400km from the Uruguayan border, it is the biggest arena in southern Brazil. Redeveloped for the tournament, it now includes an impressive roof over the seating.

RECIFE

Arena Pernambuco
CITY: Recife
CAPACITY: 44,248
MATCHES: Five, including one second round

Recife was a host city for the 1950 FIFA World Cup but it has a brand new stadium for 2014. The Pernambuco is located in the Sao Lourenco da Mata area of the city, and is part of an expansion project aimed at giving a financial boost to an area that is considered deprived. The Nautico club will move into the stadium following the tournament.

RIO DE JANEIRO

Estadio do Maracana
CITY: Rio de Janeiro
CAPACITY: 73,531
MATCHES: Seven, including the final

The Maracana is one of the most famous stadiums in the world and is the second most popular tourist attraction in Rio de Janeiro. It was once the biggest stadium in the world but has been made all-seater for the FIFA World Cup, though it remains the largest in the tournament. The bowl-like shape is iconic and has had a roof added.

SALVADOR

Arena Fonte Nova
CITY: Salvador
CAPACITY: 48,747
MATCHES: Six, including one quarter-final

Built on the site of the Estadio Octavio Mangabeira, this purpose-built modern stadium's design is based on the old ground and has been fitted with a lightweight roof covering the stands. The surrounding area includes a panoramic restaurant, museum of football, car parks, shops, hotels and a concert hall.

SAO PAULO

Arena de Sao Paulo
CITY: Sao Paulo
CAPACITY: 65,807
MATCHES: Six, including one semi-final

The 2014 FIFA World Cup will kick off in this brand new stadium, which will become the home of Brazilian giants Corinthians after the tournament. Built in the east of the city, in Itaquera, the development provided jobs for 6,000 people in a deprived region. The capacity will be reduced by 20,000 after the tournament.

A NATION'S PASSION

FIFA WORLD CUP
Brasil

Football in Brazil is not just a sport. It is not merely a game. It is a way of life. And the nation's contribution to world football goes beyond the great names on the field. The passion and vitality of Brazil's fans have become as much a part of the pageant as the yellow shirts themselves.

In a country where 50 million people live beneath the poverty line, the game provides a route out of misery for some and a vehicle for others to make sense of the social and political tensions endemic in a diverse nation. Football, it is said, brings Brazilians together, giving hope, supplying joy and providing a common theme around which they can rally.

It is why the beaches of Rio are packed on a daily basis with boys emulating their heroes, past and present, such as Pele, Zico, Ronaldo, Ronaldinho and Neymar. It is why 10,000 Brazilians are estimated to play football professionally around the world and why more than 600 play in the top leagues in Europe.

More than any other country, football in Brazil has become an integral part of the social and political framework of the nation.

The national psyche depends on whether the Selecao, the national team, wins or loses. That is a powerful notion and why Brazilians often refer to their country as 'the country of football', even though the game was introduced to the nation in the late 19th Century, quite independently, by two Scotsmen, Thomas Donohue and Charles Miller.

It was then the preserve largely of upper-class whites and Brazil only really began to forge a reputation for panache and spectacular play when the game was picked up by the black masses and became a game of the people. A game which was free and easy to play, a source of simple enjoyment which Pele, arguably the greatest player who ever lived, famously began playing with a ball made out of newspapers stuffed into socks.

The game over time became based on speed and flair and dribbling ability. Brazilians refer to it as an 'art form', while historian Gilberto Freyre wrote in 1959: "The Brazilians play football as if it were a dance."

It also became the pastime which defined the nation, especially following the national team's first FIFA World Cup triumph in 1958 in Sweden which was a celebration of the verve and vitality Brazil brought to the game.

To see how it unites the people, however, you only need to remember the hope, the pride and the togetherness it engendered when the 1970 team won the Jules Rimet trophy for the third time.

The country at the time was governed by the military and thousands of politicians had their political rights suspended. In short, the country was in turmoil. Their FIFA World Cup victory, with a team revered as the greatest in the history of the game, allowed Brazilians to look beyond the instability and unrest they had come to view as normal.

Their football fanaticism and nationalism shone through, as it did in 2013 when Brazil's route to FIFA Confederations Cup victory was accompanied by protests against a lack of investment in social services compared with spending on the World Cup and the 2016 Olympics.

The curious thing was that, as prolonged and widespread as the complaints were, they were swept away by the intense national celebrations which greeted Brazil's victory against Spain in the final.

In Brazilian culture, football is first and fervent. It impacts people individually. It affects their well-being. It drives the mood of the nation. It is why the 2014 FIFA World Cup is so important to Brazil on so many levels.

Above and opposite: Brazil fans bring colour and excitement to every game their heroes play at home and around the world.

Keisuke Honda scores from the penalty spot against as Japan clinch a 1–1 draw and become the first country, apart from the hosts, to qualify for the 2014 FIFA World Cup finals.

THE ROAD TO RIO

From the moment Brazil was chosen to host the 2014 FIFA World Cup finals, there was extra incentive to qualify for football's greatest showpiece and there was the usual mix of drama, excitement and controversy along the way as 203 teams were whittled down to the 31 who, along with the hosts, will be on show in South America.

FIFA WORLD CUP
Brasil

HOW THEY QUALIFIED

The 2014 FIFA World Cup will finish in Rio de Janeiro on July 13 and bring to an end a tournament lasting more than three years and spanning six continents. Qualifying for the World Cup finals is a special moment in any player's career and some have had to work harder than others to achieve it.

The long road to Brazil began back in June 2011 when Belize played Montserrat in front of only 150 people. Nearly two and a half years and 819 matches later, the line-up for the 2014 FIFA World Cup finals was confirmed.

Competition for all the qualifying places up for grabs was understandably fierce as every player dreamed of representing his country on football's biggest stage. Only 31 teams could join Brazil in the finals, which meant ecstasy for some and heartbreak for others.

Qualification was never really in doubt for some of world football's traditional powers but others had to fight all the way to join them.

There were fine performances from the very first game, when Deon McCaulay netted a hat-trick for Belize, right through to the latter stages when Cristiano Ronaldo's treble helped Portugal get the better of Zlatan Ibrahimovic and Sweden.

Japan were the first team to book their ticket to Brazil when Keisuke Honda's injury-time penalty against Australia secured the point they needed to clinch top spot in Asian Group B with a match to spare.

Australia were much less convincing and had to wait until their last match before Joshua Kennedy's late winner against Iraq ensured a third successive FIFA World Cup finals appearance.

Iran's defence was the key to them topping Group A, conceding just two goals in eight matches

to finish ahead of Korea Republic, who scraped through on goal difference at the expense of Uzbekistan. There was no change in fortune for Uzbekistan in the play-offs either as they suffered an agonising 9–8 penalty shootout defeat to Jordan, who advanced to another play-off against South American opposition.

That proved to be Uruguay, who were forced to take the play-off route to the finals for a fourth successive time despite Luis Suarez leading the continent's scoring chart with 11 goals. Their experience helped them hold their nerve against Jordan as a 5–0 win in the away leg effectively sealed their place in Brazil – the scene of their famous 1950 success.

Argentina made a shaky start to the South American qualifying group, including their first ever defeat to Venezuela and a home draw with Bolivia. A 2–1 win in Colombia proved the turning point and sparked a 14-match unbeaten run which ensured qualification with two matches to spare, with

Lionel Messi and Gonzalo Higuain scoring 19 goals between them.

There was tragedy too when Ecuador striker Christian Benitez died as the result of a heart problem. Chucho, as he was affectionately known, had scored four goals to put Ecuador in contention to qualify prior to his death and his team-mates showed terrific strength of character to edge out Uruguay on goal difference thanks mainly to their unbeaten home record.

Colombia and Chile produced the best match in South America as the attack-minded Chile, needing a win to qualify, surged into a three-goal lead in the second half. The home side stormed back though and rescued a 3–3 draw which saw them qualify instead, although La Roja also qualified four days later after beating Ecuador.

In Europe, the Netherlands and Germany were the pick of the nine group winners, dropping only two points each. They were joined by Belgium, Italy, Switzerland, Russia, England, Spain and Bosnia-Herzegovina, who qualified for the first time in the short history of the young nation.

France, champions in 1998, were in danger of missing out when they trailed Ukraine 2–0 after the first leg of their play-off. No European nation had previously overturned such a deficit in qualifying but on a famous night at the Stade de France, the hosts triumphed 3–0 thanks largely to a Mamadou Sakho double.

Right: Gonzalo Higuain scored nine times as Argentina recovered from a slow start to top South American qualifying and secure their place in the finals with two games to spare.

Opposite: Deon McCaulay of Belize scored the very first goals of the qualifying campaign, netting a hat-trick against Montserrat back in June 2011.

The meeting of Portugal and Sweden was billed as a showdown between two of the greatest players in the world, and Ronaldo and Ibrahimovic did not disappoint.

First blood went to the Real Madrid star, who gave Portugal a slender lead to take to Scandinavia. It looked all over when Ronaldo struck again early in the second half of the second leg but Ibrahimovic hit back with two goals in five minutes.

Sweden's joy was soon ended though as Ronaldo completed his hat-trick with two goals in three minutes to become Portugal's joint-record goalscorer and ensure he will showcase his talent on the greatest stage.

It was slightly more straightforward for the other two European qualifiers. Greece's 3–1 win in the first leg helped them overcome Romania and Iceland were denied a place at their first major finals after a 2–0 aggregate defeat to 1998 semi-finalists Croatia.

There was a strong sense of déjà vu in Africa as the five teams which qualified for the finals in South Africa in 2010 did so once again, with west African countries dominating. Only Algeria prevented a clean sweep from that region after beating Burkina Faso on away goals, with Madjid Bougherra grabbing the decisive goal as Algeria wiped out a 3–2 deficit from the first leg.

Ghana won five of their six group games and then thrashed Egypt 7–3 on aggregate. Nigeria and Cameroon were comfortable winners against Ethiopia and Tunisia respectively, while Ivory Coast were pushed all the way by Senegal before Salomon Kalou's injury-time goal completed a 4–2 aggregate success.

Mexico's stuttering form was the biggest talking point throughout the CONCACAF qualifying campaign and they were in real danger of missing out on the finals for the first time since 1990.

They were minutes away from being eliminated before being saved by two late goals from bitter rivals the USA against Panama.

That ensured Mexico claimed fourth place in the group and went through to the play-off against Oceania champions New Zealand when they finally came good with a 9–3 aggregate win.

The USA topped the CONCACAF group after bouncing back well from a surprise opening defeat in Honduras, who also produced one of the most famous results in their history with a 2–1 win in Mexico City as they finished third behind Costa Rica.

Fortunately for Mexico, the route to Brazil can now be forgotten. All that matters now is how the teams perform when they get there.

Left: Didier Drogba celebrates a goal as Ivory Coast overcome Senegal to earn their place at the FIFA World Cup finals.

AFRICA

ROUND 1

Congo	bt Sao Tome e Principe	5-0	1-1	(6-1 agg)
Namibia	bt Djibouti	4-0	4-0	(8-0 agg)
Mozambique	bt Comoro	1-0	4-1	(5-1 agg)
Rwanda	bt Eritrea	1-1	3-1	(4-2 agg)
Congo DR	bt Swaziland	3-1	5-1	(8-2 agg)
Equatorial Guinea	bt Madagascar	2-0	1-2	(3-2 agg)
Tanzania	bt Chad	2-1	0-1	(2-2 agg, away goals)
Togo	bt Guinea-Bissau	1-1	1-0	(2-1 agg)
Kenya	bt Seychelles	3-0	4-0	(7-0 agg)
Lesotho	bt Burundi	1-0	2-2	(3-2 agg)
Ethiopia	bt Somalia	0-0	5-0	(5-0 agg)

ROUND 2

GROUP A

	P	W	D	L	F	A	Pts
Ethiopia	6	4	1	1	8	6	13
South Africa	6	3	2	1	12	5	11
Botswana	6	2	1	3	8	10	7
CAR	6	1	0	5	5	12	3

GROUP B

	P	W	D	L	F	A	Pts
Tunisia	6	4	2	0	13	6	14
Cape Verde Is	6	3	0	3	9	7	9
Sierra Leone	6	2	2	2	10	10	8
Eq Guinea	6	0	2	4	6	15	2

GROUP C

	P	W	D	L	F	A	Pts
Ivory Coast	6	4	2	0	15	5	14
Morocco	6	2	3	1	9	8	9
Tanzania	6	2	0	4	8	12	6
Gambia	6	1	1	4	4	11	4

GROUP D

	P	W	D	L	F	A	Pts
Ghana	6	5	0	1	18	3	15
Zambia	6	3	2	1	11	4	11
Lesotho	6	1	2	3	4	15	5
Sudan	6	0	2	4	3	14	2

GROUP E

	P	W	D	L	F	A	Pts
Burkina Faso	6	4	0	2	7	4	12
Congo	6	3	2	1	7	3	11
Gabon	6	2	1	3	5	6	7
Niger	6	1	1	4	6	12	4

GROUP F

	P	W	D	L	F	A	Pts
Nigeria	6	3	3	0	7	3	12
Malawi	6	1	4	1	4	5	7
Kenya	6	1	3	2	4	5	6
Namibia	6	1	2	3	2	4	5

GROUP G

	P	W	D	L	F	A	Pts
Egypt	6	6	0	0	16	7	18
Guinea	6	3	1	2	12	8	10
Mozambique	6	0	3	3	2	10	3
Zimbabwe	6	0	2	4	4	9	2

GROUP H

	P	W	D	L	F	A	Pts
Algeria	6	5	0	1	13	4	15
Mali	6	2	2	2	7	7	8
Benin	6	2	2	2	8	9	8
Rwanda	6	0	2	4	3	11	2

GROUP I

	P	W	D	L	F	A	Pts
Cameroon	6	4	1	1	8	3	13
Libya	6	2	3	1	5	3	9
Congo DR	6	1	3	2	3	3	6
Togo	6	1	1	4	4	11	4

GROUP J

	P	W	D	L	F	A	Pts
Senegal	6	3	3	0	9	4	12
Uganda	6	2	2	2	5	6	8
Angola	6	1	4	1	8	6	7
Liberia	6	1	1	4	4	10	4

ROUND 3

Algeria	bt Burkina Faso	2-3	1-0	(3-3 agg, away goals)
Ivory Coast	bt Senegal	3-1	1-1	(4-2 agg)
Nigeria	bt Ethiopia	2-1	2-0	(4-1 agg)
Cameroon	bt Tunisia	0-0	4-1	(4-1 agg)
Ghana	bt Egypt	6-1	1-2	(7-3 agg)

QUALIFIED: Algeria, Cameroon, Ivory Coast, Ghana, Nigeria

SOUTH AMERICA

ROUND 1

	P	W	D	L	F	A	Pts
Argentina	16	9	5	2	35	15	32
Colombia	16	9	3	4	27	13	30
Chile	16	9	1	6	29	25	28
Ecuador	16	7	4	5	20	16	25
Uruguay	16	7	4	5	25	25	25
Venezuela	16	5	5	5	14	20	20
Peru	16	4	3	9	17	26	15
Bolivia	16	2	6	8	17	30	12
Paraguay	16	3	3	10	17	31	12

INTERCONTINENTAL PLAY-OFF

Jordan	0	Uruguay	5
Uruguay	0	Jordan	0
Uruguay won 5-0 on aggregate			

QUALIFIED

Brazil (hosts), Argentina, Colombia, Chile, Ecuador, Uruguay

Above: Lionel Messi was, as ever, the centre of attention as he led Argentina to the top of South American qualifying.

ASIA

ROUND 1

Laos	bt	Cambodia	2-4	6-2	(8-6 agg, aet)
Nepal	bt	Timor-Leste	2-1	5-0	(7-1 agg)
Palestine	bt	Afghanistan	2-0	1-1	(3-1 agg)
Philippines	bt	Sri Lanka	1-1	4-0	(5-1 agg)
Bangladesh	bt	Pakistan	3-0	0-0	(3-0 agg)
Myanmar	bt	Mongolia	0-1	2-0	(2-1 agg)
Vietnam	bt	Macau	6-0	7-1	(13-1 agg)
Malaysia	bt	Chinese Taipei	2-1	2-3	(4-4 agg, away goals)

ROUND 2

China PR	bt	Laos	7-2	6-1	(13-3 agg)
Lebanon	bt	Bangladesh	4-0	0-2	(4-2 agg)
Thailand	bt	Palestine	1-0	2-2	(3-2 agg)
Indonesia	bt	Turkmenistan	1-1	4-3	(5-4 agg)
Iraq	bt	Yemen	2-0	0-0	(2-0 agg)
Jordan	bt	Nepal	9-0	1-1	(10-1 agg)
Tajikistan	bt	Syria	3-0 awd	3-0 awd	(6-0 agg)
Uzbekistan	bt	Kyrgyzstan	4-0	3-0	(7-0 agg)
Qatar	bt	Vietnam	3-0	1-2	(4-2 agg)
Kuwait	bt	Philippines	3-0	2-1	(5-1 agg)
Iran	bt	Maldives	4-0	1-0	(5-0 agg)
Singapore	bt	Malaysia	5-3	1-1	(6-4 agg)
Oman	bt	Myanmar	2-0	2-0 awd	(4-0 agg)
United Arab Emirates	bt	India	3-0	2-2	(5-2 agg)
Saudi Arabia	bt	Hong Kong	3-0	5-0	(8-0 agg)

ROUND 3

GROUP A

	P	W	D	L	F	A	Pts
Iraq	6	5	0	1	14	4	15
Jordan	6	4	0	2	11	7	12
China PR	6	3	0	3	10	6	9
Singapore	6	0	0	6	2	20	0

GROUP B

	P	W	D	L	F	A	Pts
Korea Rep	6	4	1	1	14	4	13
Lebanon	6	3	1	2	10	14	10
Kuwait	6	2	2	2	8	9	8
UAE	6	1	0	5	9	14	3

GROUP C

	P	W	D	L	F	A	Pts
Uzbekistan	6	5	1	0	8	1	16
Japan	6	3	1	2	14	3	10
Korea DPR	6	2	1	3	3	4	7
Tajikistan	6	0	1	5	1	18	1

GROUP D

	P	W	D	L	F	A	Pts
Australia	6	5	0	1	13	5	15
Oman	6	2	2	2	3	6	8
Saudi Arabia	6	1	3	2	6	7	6
Thailand	6	1	1	4	4	8	4

GROUP E

	P	W	D	L	F	A	Pts
Iran	6	3	3	0	17	5	12
Qatar	6	2	4	0	10	5	10
Bahrain	6	2	3	1	13	7	9
Indonesia	6	0	0	6	3	26	0

ROUND 4

GROUP A

	P	W	D	L	F	A	Pts
Iran	8	5	1	2	8	2	16
Korea Rep	8	4	2	2	13	7	14
Uzbekistan	8	4	2	2	11	6	14
Qatar	8	2	1	5	5	13	7
Lebanon	8	1	2	5	3	12	5

GROUP B

	P	W	D	L	F	A	Pts
Japan	8	5	2	1	16	5	17
Australia	8	3	4	1	12	7	13
Jordan	8	3	1	4	7	16	10
Oman	8	2	3	3	7	10	9
Iraq	8	1	2	5	4	8	5

ROUND 5

Jordan	1	Uzbekistan	1
Uzbekistan	1	Jordan	1

2-2 on aggregate, Jordan won 9-8 on pens

INTERCONTINENTAL PLAY-OFF

Jordan	0	Uruguay	5
Uruguay	0	Jordan	0

Uruguay won 5-0 on aggregate

QUALIFIED
Australia, Iran, Japan, Korea Republic

Above: Japan and Australia both qualified for the FIFA World Cup finals despite being drawn together at the final group stage of Asia qualifying.

EUROPE

ROUND 1

GROUP A

	P	W	D	L	F	A	Pts
Belgium	10	8	2	0	18	4	26
Croatia	10	5	2	3	12	9	17
Serbia	10	4	2	4	18	11	14
Scotland	10	3	2	5	8	12	11
Wales	10	3	1	6	9	20	10
Macedonia	10	2	1	7	7	16	7

GROUP B

	P	W	D	L	F	A	Pts
Italy	10	6	4	0	19	9	22
Denmark	10	4	4	2	17	12	16
Czech Rep	10	4	3	3	13	9	15
Bulgaria	10	3	4	3	14	9	13
Armenia	10	4	1	5	12	13	13
Malta	10	1	0	9	5	28	3

GROUP C

	P	W	D	L	F	A	Pts
Germany	10	9	1	0	36	10	28
Sweden	10	6	2	2	19	14	20
Austria	10	5	2	3	20	10	17
Rep Ireland	10	4	2	4	16	17	14
Kazakhstan	10	1	2	7	6	21	5
Faroe Is	10	0	1	9	4	29	1

GROUP D

	P	W	D	L	F	A	Pts
Netherlands	10	9	1	0	34	5	28
Romania	10	6	1	3	19	12	19
Hungary	10	5	2	3	21	20	17
Turkey	10	5	1	4	16	9	16
Estonia	10	2	1	7	6	20	7
Andorra	10	0	0	10	0	30	0

GROUP E

	P	W	D	L	F	A	Pts
Switzerland	10	7	3	0	17	6	24
Iceland	10	5	2	3	17	15	17
Slovenia	10	5	0	5	14	11	15
Norway	10	3	3	4	10	13	12
Albania	10	3	2	5	9	11	11
Cyprus	10	1	2	7	4	15	5

GROUP F

	P	W	D	L	F	A	Pts
Russia	10	7	1	2	20	5	22
Portugal	10	6	3	1	20	9	21
Israel	10	3	5	2	19	14	14
Azerbaijan	10	1	6	3	7	11	9
N Ireland	10	1	4	5	9	17	7
Luxembourg	10	1	3	6	7	26	6

GROUP G

	P	W	D	L	F	A	Pts
Bosnia-H	10	8	1	1	30	6	25
Greece	10	8	1	1	12	4	25
Slovakia	10	3	4	3	11	10	13
Lithuania	10	3	2	5	9	11	11
Latvia	10	2	2	6	10	20	8
Liechtenstein	10	0	2	8	4	25	2

GROUP H

	P	W	D	L	F	A	Pts
England	10	6	4	0	31	4	22
Ukraine	10	6	3	1	28	4	21
Montenegro	10	4	3	3	18	17	15
Poland	10	3	4	3	18	12	13
Moldova	10	3	2	5	12	17	11
San Marino	10	0	0	10	1	54	0

GROUP I

	P	W	D	L	F	A	Pts
Spain	8	6	2	0	14	3	20
France	8	5	2	1	15	6	17
Finland	8	2	3	3	5	9	9
Georgia	8	1	2	5	3	10	5
Belarus	8	1	1	6	7	16	4

Above: Mesut Ozil was leading scorer with seven of Germany's 36 goals in qualifying, the most of any European nation on the road to Brazil. Their nine wins and a draw was matched only by old rivals Netherlands in European qualifying.

ROUND 2

Iceland	0	Croatia	0
Croatia	2	Iceland	0

Croatia won 2-0 on aggregate

Portugal	1	Sweden	0
Sweden	2	Portugal	3

Portugal won 4-2 on aggregate

Ukraine	2	France	0
France	3	Ukraine	0

France won 3-2 on aggregate

Greece	3	Romania	1
Romania	1	Greece	0

Greece won 4-2 on aggregate

QUALIFIED

Belgium, Bosnia-Herzegovina, England, Germany, Italy, Netherlands, Russia, Spain, Switzerland. Croatia, Portugal, France, Greece

Left: The United States and Costa Rica clash on their way to the top places in the final group of CONCACAF qualifying.

NORTH, CENTRAL AMERICA AND CARIBBEAN

ROUND 1

Belize	bt Montserrat	5-2	3-1	(8-3 agg)
Bahamas	bt Turks and Caicos Islands	4-0	6-0	(10-0 agg)
US Virgin Islands	bt British Virgin Islands	2-0	2-1	(4-1 agg)
Dominican Republic	bt Anguilla	2-0	4-0	(6-0 agg)
St Lucia	bt Aruba	2-4	4-2	(6-6 agg, 5-4 pens)

ROUND 2

GROUP A

	P	W	D	L	F	A	Pts
El Salvador	6	6	0	0	20	5	18
Dominican Rep	6	2	2	2	12	8	8
Suriname	6	2	1	3	5	11	7
Cayman Is	6	0	1	5	2	15	1

GROUP B

	P	W	D	L	F	A	Pts
Guyana	6	4	1	1	9	6	13
Trinidad & T	6	4	0	2	12	4	12
Bermuda	6	3	1	2	8	7	10
Barbados	6	0	0	6	2	14	0

GROUP C

	P	W	D	L	F	A	Pts
Panama	4	4	0	0	15	2	12
Nicaragua	4	2	0	2	5	7	6
Dominica	4	0	0	4	0	11	0

GROUP D

	P	W	D	L	F	A	Pts
Canada	6	4	2	0	18	1	14
Puerto Rico	6	2	3	1	8	4	9
St Kitts & Nevis	6	1	4	1	6	8	7
St Lucia	6	0	1	5	4	23	1

GROUP E

	P	W	D	L	F	A	Pts
Guatemala	6	6	0	0	19	3	18
Belize	6	2	1	3	9	10	7
St Vincent/Grenadines	6	1	2	3	4	12	5
Grenada	6	1	1	4	7	14	4

GROUP F

	P	W	D	L	F	A	Pts
Antigua & Barbuda	6	5	0	1	28	5	15
Haiti	6	4	1	1	21	6	13
Curacao	6	2	1	3	15	15	7
US Virgin Is	6	0	0	6	2	40	0

ROUND 3

GROUP A

	P	W	D	L	F	A	Pts
USA	6	4	1	1	11	6	13
Jamaica	6	3	1	2	9	6	10
Guatemala	6	3	1	2	9	8	10
Antigua & Barbuda	6	0	1	5	4	13	1

GROUP B

	P	W	D	L	F	A	Pts
Mexico	6	6	0	0	15	2	18
Costa Rica	6	3	1	2	14	5	10
El Salvador	6	1	2	3	8	11	5
Guyana	6	0	1	5	5	24	1

GROUP C

	P	W	D	L	F	A	Pts
Honduras	6	3	2	1	12	3	11
Panama	6	3	2	1	6	2	11
Canada	6	3	1	2	6	10	10
Cuba	6	0	1	5	1	10	1

ROUND 4

	P	W	D	L	F	A	Pts
USA	10	7	1	2	15	8	22
Costa Rica	10	5	3	2	13	7	18
Honduras	10	4	3	3	13	12	15
Mexico	10	2	5	3	7	9	11
Panama	10	1	5	4	10	14	8
Jamaica	10	0	5	5	5	13	5

INTERCONTINENTAL PLAY-OFF

New Zealand	2	Mexico	4
Mexico	5	New Zealand	1

Mexico won 9-3 on aggregate

QUALIFIED

USA, Costa Rica, Honduras, Mexico

OCEANIA

ROUND 1

	P	W	D	L	F	A	Pts
Samoa	3	2	1	0	5	3	7
Tonga	3	1	1	1	4	4	4
American Samoa	3	1	1	1	3	3	4
Cook Islands	3	0	1	2	4	6	1

ROUND 2

GROUP A

	P	W	D	L	F	A	Pts
Tahiti	3	3	0	0	18	5	9
New Caledonia	3	2	0	1	17	6	6
Vanuatu	3	1	0	2	8	9	3
Samoa	3	0	0	3	1	24	0

GROUP B

	P	W	D	L	F	A	Pts
New Zealand	3	2	1	0	4	2	7
Solomon Is	3	1	2	0	2	1	5
Fiji	3	0	2	1	1	2	2
PNG	3	0	1	2	2	4	1

ROUND 3

	P	W	D	L	F	A	Pts
New Zealand	6	6	0	0	17	2	18
New Caledonia	6	4	0	2	17	6	12
Tahiti	6	1	0	5	2	12	3
Solomon Is	6	1	0	5	5	21	3

INTERCONTINENTAL PLAY-OFF

New Zealand	2	Mexico	4
Mexico	5	New Zealand	1

Mexico won 9-3 on aggregate

THE FINAL DRAW

FIFA WORLD CUP
Brasil

The excitement over a forthcoming FIFA World Cup goes up a level once the draw is made and that was certainly the case once the fixture schedule for Brazil 2014 was confirmed at a ceremony at the Costa do Sauipe resort in December.

All eyes were on the luxurious Costa do Sauipe resort on 6 December as the draw for Brazil 2014 was conducted by a host of star names on the beautiful coast of Bahia.

Legends of the game Cafu, Fabio Cannavaro, Alcides Ghiggia, Fernando Hierro, Sir Geoff Hurst, Mario Kempes, Lothar Matthaus and Zinedine Zidane represented eight previous winners and joined FIFA Secretary General Jerome Valcke and hostess Fernanda

Lima in the north-east of the host country.

With 1,300 guests, more than 2,000 media representatives and a huge television audience watching from almost 200 countries, the 32 competing nations were drawn into eight groups, with two teams to qualify from each section.

FIFA rankings dictated that Argentina, Colombia, Uruguay, Belgium, Germany, Spain and Switzerland would join Brazil as top seeds, with the other countries

split into three separate pots based on geographic considerations.

With the European section overloaded with nine entries, an additional ballot took place to see which team would be switched to the Africa and South America list, with Italy the nation emerging from this process.

Brazil were then automatically installed in Group A and after opening the tournament with a clash against Croatia at the Arena Corinthians in Sao Paulo, the hosts will also face Mexico and Cameroon as they go in search of a sixth FIFA World Cup triumph.

Group B saw 2010 FIFA World Cup South Africa finalists Spain and the Netherlands paired together, with exciting South American side Chile and the always dangerous Australia joining them in a tough section.

As the runners-up from that quartet will face the Group A table toppers, *La Roja* coach Vicente del Bosque admitted securing first place could be crucial to progressing into the later rounds of the tournament. "We were hoping to have a less difficult group," he commented. "I expect that Brazil will finish first and so we have to give everything to make sure we win our group, too."

However, Chile manager Jorge Sampaoli declared: "Forget about Brazil! First you have to qualify and this is a very tough group. We're not afraid of anybody, though."

Three previous FIFA World Cup winners were drawn out in Group D,

with Uruguay, England and Italy being joined by Costa Rica in another daunting pool.

"You don't see three world champions together every day, but that's exactly what makes a World Cup so special," said Azzurri coach Cesare Prandelli.

"It's the biggest football party there is and, as such, it's where you find the biggest teams."

England chief Roy Hodgson added: "Our opponents have got world-class players; Suarez is a top player, so are Cavani, Balotelli and Pirlo. However, I like to think there are two or three players in our team who are at the same level and that Italy and Uruguay are starting to think about Gerrard, Rooney and Co."

Group G could see another family reunion for Germany defender Jerome Boateng and his half-brother Kevin-Prince Boateng, of Ghana, who became the first siblings to do battle at a FIFA World Cup four years ago.

With Cristiano Ronaldo's Portugal and the Jurgen Klinsmann-managed USA also present, there will be no shortage of talking points in this section. Current Germany coach Joachim Low was Klinsmann's right-hand man when that nation hosted the finals in 2006 and he said: "Of course, the reunion with Jurgen is very special. We're also up against Ghana, who we played against at the 2010 World Cup in South Africa, and the challenge of facing Portugal with Cristiano Ronaldo also has its appeal."

Klinsmann commented: "It's one of the most difficult groups of the whole draw, but hopefully we'll surprise some people in Brazil."

Above: Dancers perform on stage during the entertainment at the Draw ceremony.

Opposite: Former Brazil striker Bebeto reprises his famous goal celebration with the tournament mascot Fuleco.

GROUP A
June 12, 9pm, Sao Paulo
Brazil ....
Croatia ....

June 13, 5pm, Natal
Mexico ....
Cameroon ....

June 17, 8pm, Fortaleza
Brazil ....
Mexico ....

June 18, 11pm, Manaus
Cameroon ....
Croatia ....

June 23, 9pm, Brasilia
Cameroon ....
Brazil ....

June 23, 9pm, Recife
Croatia ....
Mexico ....

GROUP A TABLE

	P	W	D	L	F	A	Pts
1	3						
2	3						
3	3						
4	3						

GROUP B
June 13, 8pm, Salvador
Spain ....
Netherlands ....

June 13, 11pm, Cuiaba
Chile ....
Australia ....

June 18, 8pm, Rio de Janeiro
Spain ....
Chile ....

June 18, 5pm, Porto Alegre
Australia ....
Netherlands ....

June 23, 5pm, Curitiba
Australia ....
Spain ....

June 23, 5pm, Sao Paulo
Netherlands ....
Chile ....

GROUP B TABLE

	P	W	D	L	F	A	Pts
1	3						
2	3						
3	3						
4	3						

GROUP C
June 14, 5pm, Belo Horizonte
Colombia ....
Greece ....

June 15, 2am, Recife
Ivory Coast ....
Japan ....

June 19, 5pm, Brasilia
Colombia ....
Ivory Coast ....

June 19, 11pm, Natal
Japan ....
Greece ....

June 24, 9pm, Cuiaba
Japan ....
Colombia ....

June 24, 9pm, Fortaleza
Greece ....
Ivory Coast ....

GROUP C TABLE

	P	W	D	L	F	A	Pts
1	3						
2	3						
3	3						
4	3						

GROUP G
June 16, 5pm, Salvador
Germany ....
Portugal ....

June 16, 11pm, Natal
Ghana ....
United States ....

June 21, 8pm, Fortaleza
Germany ....
Ghana ....

June 22, 11pm, Manaus
United States ....
Portugal ....

June 26, 5pm, Recife
United States ....
Germany ....

June 26, 5pm, Brasilia
Portugal ....
Ghana ....

GROUP G TABLE

	P	W	D	L	F	A	Pts
1	3						
2	3						
3	3						
4	3						

GROUP H
June 17, 5pm, Belo Horizonte
Belgium ....
Algeria ....

June 17, 11pm, Cuiaba
Russia ....
Korea Republic ....

June 22, 5pm, Rio de Janeiro
Belgium ....
Russia ....

June 22, 8pm, Porto Alegre
Korea Republic ....
Algeria ....

June 26, 9pm, Sao Paulo
Korea Republic ....
Belgium ....

June 26, 9pm, Curitiba
Algeria ....
Russia ....

GROUP H TABLE

	P	W	D	L	F	A	Pts
1	3						
2	3						
3	3						
4	3						

ROUND OF 16
1. June 28, 5pm, Belo Horizonte
Winner A ....
Runner-up B ....

2. June 28, 9pm, Rio de Janeiro
Winner C ....
Runner-up D ....

3. June 29, 5pm, Fortaleza
Winner B ....
Runner-up A ....

4. June 29, 9pm, Recife
Winner D ....
Runner-up C ....

5. June 30, 5pm, Brasilia
Winner E ....
Runner-up F ....

6. June 30, 9pm, Porto Alegre
Winner G ....
Runner-up H ....

7. July 1, 5pm, Sao Paulo
Winner F ....
Runner-up E ....

8. July 1, 9pm, Salvador
Winner H ....
Runner-up G ....

GROUP D

June 14, 8pm, Fortaleza
Uruguay....................................
Costa Rica...............................

June 14, 11pm, Manaus
England....................................
Italy...

June 19, 8pm, Sao Paulo
Uruguay....................................
England....................................

June 20, 5pm, Recife
Italy...
Costa Rica...............................

June 24, 5pm, Natal
Italy...
Uruguay....................................

June 24, 5pm, Belo Horizonte
Costa Rica...............................
England....................................

GROUP D TABLE

	P	W	D	L	F	A	Pts
1	3						
2	3						
3	3						
4	3						

GROUP E

June 15, 5pm, Brasilia
Switzerland..............................
Ecuador...................................

June 15, 8pm, Porto Alegre
France......................................
Honduras..................................

June 20, 8pm, Salvador
Switzerland..............................
France......................................

June 20, 11pm, Curitiba
Honduras..................................
Ecuador...................................

June 25, 9pm, Manaus
Honduras..................................
Switzerland..............................

June 25, 9pm, Rio de Janeiro
Ecuador...................................
France......................................

GROUP E TABLE

	P	W	D	L	F	A	Pts
1	3						
2	3						
3	3						
4	3						

GROUP F

June 15, 11pm, Rio de Janeiro
Argentina.................................
Bosnia-Herzegovina................

June 16, 8pm, Curitiba
Iran...
Nigeria.....................................

June 21, 5pm, Belo Horizonte
Argentina.................................
Iran...

June 21, 11pm, Cuiaba
Nigeria.....................................
Bosnia-Herzegovina................

June 25, 5pm, Porto Alegre
Nigeria.....................................
Argentina.................................

June 25, 5pm, Salvador
Bosnia-Herzegovina................
Iran...

GROUP F TABLE

	P	W	D	L	F	A	Pts
1	3						
2	3						
3	3						
4	3						

QUARTER-FINALS

A. July 4, 9pm, Fortaleza
Winner 1...................................
Winner 2...................................

B. July 4, 5pm, Rio de Janeiro
Winner 5...................................
Winner 6...................................

C. July 5, 9pm, Salvador
Winner 3...................................
Winner 4...................................

D. July 5, 5pm, Brasilia
Winner 7...................................
Winner 8...................................

SEMI-FINALS

July 8, 9pm, Belo Horizonte
Winner A...................................
Winner B...................................

July 9, 9pm, Sao Paulo
Winner C...................................
Winner D...................................

3rd/4th PLAY-OFF

July 12, 9pm, Brasilia
....
....

FIFA WORLD CUP FINAL

July 13, 8pm, Rio de Janeiro
....
....

All kick-off times are shown in
British Summer Time

FIFA WORLD CUP
Brasil

Spain players and officials celebrate after winning the 2010 FIFA World Cup in Johannesburg. Now they defend their title in Brazil with 31 other nations out to stop them.

MEET THE TEAMS

Competing at the FIFA World Cup finals is the pinnacle of a footballer's career and 31 teams have come through qualifying to earn the right to join hosts Brazil in the latest edition of the tournament. Some players preparing to strut their stuff are already global superstars while others are lesser known but now have the opportunity to showcase their talent in front of a global audience.

FIFA WORLD CUP
Brasil

BRAZIL

THE SAMBA BOYS

Brazil have won the FIFA World Cup a record five times but it would be extra special if they were to triumph on home soil. The host nation may not be the force that they once were, but they will be hoping that coach Luiz Felipe Scolari has the Midas touch once again.

There is always a weight of expectation on Brazil to win the FIFA World Cup but seldom will a nation be under more pressure to lift the famous trophy than the Samba Boys on home soil.

COACH

LUIZ FELIPE SCOLARI

There are not many coaches with more experience than Luiz Felipe ("Big Phil") Scolari and he will carry the hopes of a football-mad nation at the 2014 FIFA World Cup.

Scolari led Brazil to FIFA World Cup glory in Japan and Korea in 2002 and the 65-year-old will be looking to repeat that feat after he was appointed as coach of the Samba Boys for a second time in November 2012.

One of the most colourful characters in the game, Scolari was Portugal coach from 2003 to 2008, and he has more than 30 years' experience managing at club level.

The South American country are among the heavyweights in world football, having been crowned world champions no less than five times – more than any other country.

Renowned for their flair, silky skills and outstanding natural ability, Brazil are usually among the favourites heading into major tournaments and it will be no different when they bid to become world champions for a sixth time.

Brazil teams in years gone by have had an aura of invincibility about them, but they have not been the dominant force in recent years.

In each of the last two FIFA World Cups, Brazil have gone out at the quarter-final stage and they also failed to progress beyond the last eight at the 2011 Copa America.

It has been a period of transition for Brazil in recent years, but coach Luiz Felipe Scolari is confident that he can produce a winning formula when it matters most.

Scolari said: "I want Brazil fans to know we are building a strong team.

"Everyone knows there are no shortcuts for success, you need to win in stages and we have to go to each stage to reach the final goal."

Scolari is vastly experienced and knows what it takes to win a FIFA World Cup, having masterminded

Left to right: Brazil: (top row) Dani Alves, Julio Cesar, Ramires, Dante, Luis Fabiano, David Luiz; (bottom row) Ronaldinho, Paulinho, Adriano, Neymar, Oscar.

STAR MAN

NEYMAR

(Neymar da Silva Santos Junior)
BORN: 5 February 1992
CLUB: Barcelona (Spain)

Neymar has been billed as the next big thing for some time and there would be no better time for the Brazil prodigy to come of age than at the 2014 FIFA World Cup.

Possessing the outstanding natural talent that we have almost come to expect from young players emerging from a country that is such a hotbed of football, Neymar is one of the most talked-about footballers on the planet.

He increased his profile further with a lucrative move to Barcelona in the summer of 2013 and the skilful Samba star will be looking to take centre stage in his first FIFA World Cup.

BRAZIL AT THE FIFA WORLD CUP™

1930	1st round
1934	1st round
1938	3rd place
1950	runners-up
1954	quarter-finals
1958	CHAMPIONS
1962	CHAMPIONS
1966	1st round
1970	CHAMPIONS
1974	4th place
1978	3rd place
1982	2nd round
1986	quarter-finals
1990	round of 16
1994	CHAMPIONS
1998	runners-up
2002	CHAMPIONS
2006	quarter-finals
2010	quarter-finals

Brazil's last triumph, in Japan and South Korea back in 2002.

The charismatic 65-year-old is a wily tactician with more than 30 years in management under his belt and his experience will be vital, particularly his man-management of precious talents such as Neymar.

The former Santos forward has been hailed as one to watch for some time, and all eyes will be on the naturally gifted Barcelona player.

And Neymar has no doubt Scolari is the right man to lead Brazil in the second FIFA World Cup to be held in the country.

He said: "The players love having Scolari as coach. We all respect him – but it works two ways. He is the sort of man that if you show him respect, he will show you respect.

"Already he is coming up with new ideas about how we can improve. He is very clear that only winning the World Cup will do."

Scolari will put his faith in young players such as Neymar, Chelsea midfielder Oscar and Paris Saint-Germain starlet Lucas Moura, and their success at the FIFA Confederations Cup Brazil 2013 suggested they have the right mix of youth and experience.

Brazil are never short of attacking talent, but they are not renowned for their ability to keep the back door shut, so captain Thiago Silva will be important at the heart of their defence as they look to make the most of home advantage and ensure the FIFA World Cup is not won by a European nation for a third consecutive occasion.

Brazil fans have had plenty to celebrate down the years, but winning the FIFA World Cup in their own backyard would spark a party to end all parties.

ONES TO WATCH

LUCAS MOURA (Lucas Rodrigues Moura da Silva)
BORN: 13 August 1992
CLUB: Paris St Germain (France)

An attack-minded winger with exceptional pace, Lucas Moura has been a revelation since joining Paris Saint-Germain in January 2013. The talented 21-year-old has the rare ability to quickly turn defence into attack, reminiscent of Cristiano Ronaldo in his early years, and will complement Neymar and Oscar in a mouth-watering front three.

THIAGO SILVA (Thiago Emiliano da Silva)
BORN: 22 September 1984
CLUB: Paris St Germain (France)

Brazil have always had an array of attacking talent, but for them to succeed it is vital they keep things tight at the back and captain Thiago Silva is an inspiration at the heart of the Samba Boys' defence. Strong in the air and very comfortable with the ball on the ground, the Paris St Germain centre-back is one of the best defenders in world football.

CROATIA

FIFA WORLD CUP
Brasil

THE VATRENI

Igor Stimac was removed as coach after Croatia finished second in their qualifying group, with former captain Niko Kovac taking charge and negotiating a play-off against Iceland. Now he has the task of getting through to the knockout stages of the finals for the first time since 1998.

COACH

NIKO KOVAC

As a player, former captain Niko Kovac was seconds away from leading Croatia to a first ever European Championship semi-final in 2008 before an eventual penalty shootout defeat to Turkey.

Now, as a coach, he will hope to take Croatia through the group stages at the FIFA World Cup finals for the first time since 1998. He replaced former team-mate Igor Stimac at the helm of the national team after Croatia stuttered into the play-offs. Despite his only other managerial job being with the nation's U-21 side, Kovac negotiated the two-legged tie with Iceland to book their spot in Brazil, where he will face his biggest challenge since hanging up his boots.

Croatia's class of 1998 certainly set the bar high for the players tasked with following in their footsteps but that is the challenge facing the current squad.

Croatia made their maiden FIFA World Cup finals appearance at France 1998 when the Davor Suker-inspired team finished third after a fairytale run to the semi-finals, but their campaigns in 2002 and 2006 did not last beyond the first round and they did not qualify for 2010.

Now, with the legendary Niko Kovac at the helm, confidence is high that they can progress to the knockout stages in Brazil, a country that the new coach feels is a fitting venue. "It will be a spectacular tournament," said Kovac. "A World Cup is always a spectacle anyway. It's a football-mad country, it'll be non-stop football, 24 hours a day. It's far away from Europe and we are bound to have to adjust a little but I'm looking forward to it."

Kovac, a tough, uncompromising midfielder in his playing days, missed out on the 1998 FIFA World Cup finals through injury but featured in both of Croatia's other two appearances.

He scored 14 goals in 83 appearances for his country, and offered protection to the defence to allow the flair players to perform going forward.

Croatia continue to have an abundance of attacking players but

Left to right: Croatia: (top row) Josip Simunic, Mario Mandzukic, Vedran Corluka, Ivan Rakitic, Stipe Pletikosa, Ivan Perisic; (bottom row) Darijo Srna, Mateo Kovacic, Luka Modric, Danijel Pranjic, Ivica Olic.

STAR MAN

LUKA MODRIC

BORN: 9 September 1985
CLUB: Real Madrid (Spain)

The diminutive playmaker has morphed from a 'number 10' into an all-round central midfielder who stamps his authority on a game. Deceptively strong for such a slight frame, Luka Modric can stand up to a physical battle and is also capable of playing telling passes from deep.

He recovered from a slow start to become a key player at Real Madrid since joining from Tottenham Hotspur in 2012.

For his country, he is a vitally important player, tasked with setting the tempo in midfield and breaking forward to link up with the strikers. If Modric plays well, Croatia will be a force.

In defence, captain Darijo Srna will get forward regularly from right-back and Danijel Pranjic will do the same on the left. That leaves the central defenders with a lot of responsibility and Kovac has the option of the experienced Vedran Corluka or the maturing Dejan Lovren.

Croatia will need to improve on their qualifying campaign when they were beaten home and away by Scotland, were second best to Belgium and failed to win any of their last four group games, but Kovac is confident he can make that happen.

"I have a clear concept of how we should play and we have the players to implement the gameplan," he said. "I want Croatia to be mobile in defence and creative in attack. This is my concept of football and now that we have qualified for the World Cup, we must start nurturing this style at grass-root level."

If Kovac gets his wish, Croatia could well be one of the most eye-catching teams in Brazil.

are missing someone in Kovac's ilk to sit back and keep things tight. During qualifying, the likes of Ivan Rakitic and Mateo Kovacic were at times deployed as a holding midfielder but both prefer playing further forward.

It is likely Ognjen Vukojevic will be tasked with the disciplined role in the finals, allowing Real Madrid star Luka Modric the freedom to take control of the game in midfield.

Further forward, Bayern Munich striker Mario Mandzukic was the top scorer in qualifying but will sit out the start of the tournament through suspension, having received a red card in the second leg of the play-off win against Iceland.

Kovac is disappointed to be without his first-choice striker but is confident the Vatreni can continue to impress in his absence.

"Mandzukic is obviously a very important player for us but we have a system in which other options can fit in if he is unavailable," said Kovac. "We will keep playing attacking football based on keeping possession and work hard to improve in every department."

Nikica Jelavic will likely fill the void in the opening games, with Eduardo and veteran Ivica Olic also hoping to be involved, while three from Rakitic, Kovacic, Niko Kranjcar, Ivo Ilicevic and Ivan Perisic are expected to start in attacking midfield positions.

ONES TO WATCH

MATEO KOVACIC

BORN: 6 May 1994
CLUB: Inter Milan (Italy)

The talented youngster made his international debut as a holding midfielder in the 2–0 win over Serbia during qualifying but is more commonly found in an advanced position for club side Inter Milan. He likes to run at defenders and has a great turn of pace, and could announce himself to the world in Brazil.

DEJAN LOVREN

BORN: 5 July 1989
CLUB: Southampton (England)

With veteran Josip Simunic suspended, Dejan Lovren will be looked upon to keep the Croatia defence tight in Brazil. After two-and-a-half seasons in Ligue 1 with Lyon, the centre-back moved to the English Premier League at the start of the 2013–14 season and immediately impressed for Southampton.

MEXICO

EL TRI

Mexico had to go through four managers and a near 14,000-mile round trip to New Zealand to reach Brazil 2014 after a troubled qualifying campaign, but will be hoping to recapture the sparkle of their gold-medal success at the London 2012 Olympics when the action begins.

COACH

MIGUEL HERRERA

Brought in to get Mexico through a play-off against New Zealand, Miguel Herrera showed he is very much his own man and not afraid to make tough decisions when relying on home-based players ahead of more established names based in Europe.

The gamble paid off in impressive fashion, but he is no stranger to making bold moves, having led club side America to their 11th league championship after declaring when landing that job: "If in six months I don't give results, I leave."

A 14-times capped defender in his playing days, Herrera will bring a disciplined and realistic approach to an *El Tri* squad perhaps guilty of over-confidence earlier in their qualifying campaign.

Mexico had to survive an almighty scare before finally booking their place in the FIFA World Cup finals for the 15th time. *El Tri* usually cruise through the CONCACAF qualifying campaign but this time had to come through a play-off with New Zealand following a series of setbacks.

Estadio Azteca has traditionally been a fortress, with Mexico having 100,000 passionate fans behind them as well as the benefit of playing at high altitude.

However, this time their home form deserted them, with October's 2–1 defeat of Panama, courtesy of Raul Jimenez's late goal, being a first victory in Mexico City after three goalless draws and a shock loss to Honduras, only

their second in 78 such games at that venue. A closing defeat in Costa Rica meant *El Tri* still had to rely on bitter rivals USA beating Panama to claim fourth spot in the table and that play-off reprieve, with the Americans coming from behind to win 3–2 thanks to a couple of injury-time goals.

Past differences with their neighbours were put to one side as Mexican television commentator Christian Martinoli screamed: "We love you! We love you forever and ever! God Bless America!"

US Soccer also tweeted #YoureWelcomeMexico and *El Tri* took full advantage of their second chance when thrashing the Kiwis 5–1 at home and 4–2 in Wellington to finally book a trip to Brazil.

Left to right: Mexico: (top row) Hugo Ayala, Guillermo Ochoa, Rafael Marquez, Jorge Torres, Oribe Peralta, Jesus Zavala; (bottom row) Christian Gimenez, Carlos Pena, Miguel Layun, Javier Aquino, Javier Hernandez.

STAR MAN

JAVIER HERNANDEZ

(Javier Hernandez Balcazar)
BORN: 1 June 1988
CLUB: Manchester United (England)
With a father and grandfather who represented Mexico at FIFA World Cup finals in 1986 and 1954 respectively, Javier Hernandez was born to the role, and upheld family honour when competing at South Africa 2010, scoring against France and Argentina.

A record of 26 goals in 64 games for Guadalajara had already alerted Manchester United, who snapped him up before that tournament and Chicharito has continued to prove a lethal marksman when given the chance.

He topped the scoring charts when Mexico won the 2011 CONCACAF Gold Cup.

MEXICO AT THE FIFA WORLD CUP™

1930	1st round
1950	1st round
1954	1st round
1958	1st round
1962	1st round
1966	1st round
1970	Quarter-finals
1978	1st round
1986	Quarter-finals
1994	Round of 16
1998	Round of 16
2002	Round of 16
2006	Round of 16
2010	Round of 16

Remarkably, Mexico had four coaches in the final stages of their road to Rio, with Jose Manuel Chepo de la Torre sacked after the loss to Honduras, his assistant Jose Luis Tena was promoted for one match and Victor Manuel Vucetich went two games later.

Miguel Herrera then steadied the ship in a slightly unconventional manner, leaving out all overseas stars such as Manchester United's Javier Hernandez and Giovani dos Santos of Villarreal in favour of home-based players. The Club America coach's approach paid off, though, with Santos Laguna striker Oribe Peralta scoring two in Mexico City and a hat-trick in New Zealand to get El Tri back on track.

Club Leon midfielder Luis Montes commented: "The fact is we all feel very comfortable with Miguel. He has a tremendous amount of confidence in us and I think that's been the secret.

"His ideas are very clear and that's allowed us to start playing good football again. We close down the opposition well, we keep on running and we create a lot of

chances. We wouldn't be in the position we're in without him."

It remains to be seen whether Mexico will be able to re-integrate some of their bigger names for the finals, but anyone ready to write them off as fortunate qualifiers expected to struggle in Brazil would do well to remember their stunning success at the London 2012 Olympics. Peralta was again the hero when scoring twice in a 2-1 Wembley win over Brazil which

saw his side strike gold, with star names such as Neymar, Oscar and Hulk in the opposition that day.

Mexico have also reached the knockout stages at the last five FIFA World Cups and a proud history includes getting to the quarter-finals in 1970 and 1986, both times as hosts.

They will not have the luxury of home advantage this time, but perhaps after all their recent trials and tribulations, getting away from it all may give them the best chance of success. Whether it is established European club stars such as Hernandez, Dos Santos and Andres Guardado or local heroes like Peralta, Jimenez and Carlos Pena leading the way is another question altogether.

ONES TO WATCH

ORIBE PERALTA

(Oribe Peralta Morones)
BORN: 12 January 1984
CLUB: Santos Laguna (Mexico)
Oribe Peralta has been Mexico's most prolific forward in recent years, top scoring in their 2011 Pan American Games success, netting twice as El Tri beat Brazil in the 2012 Olympics gold-medal match and destroying New Zealand in their FIFA World Cup qualifying play-off.

GIOVANI DOS SANTOS

(Giovani dos Santos Ramirez)
BORN: 11 May 1989
CLUB: Villarreal (Spain)
A versatile playmaker who can be deployed as a second striker or attacking midfielder, Giovani dos Santos has already built up a wealth of experience. Despite only being in his mid-20s, he has already represented Barcelona, Tottenham Hotspur, Mallorca and Villarreal at club level.

CAMEROON

FIFA WORLD CUP
Brasil

THE INDOMITABLE LIONS

West Germany may have won the 1990 FIFA World Cup but Cameroon stole the show. The Indomitable Lions beat holders Argentina on their way to the quarter-finals as Roger Milla's hip-wiggling dancing saw him become a legend. Could a new Cameroon star be born in Brazil?

COACH

VOLKER FINKE

Volker Finke took over as Cameroon coach in May 2012 and successfully hit his first target of getting the team to Brazil. The next objective will be to improve on previous tournaments, which would mean reaching the last 16.

The German, who managed SC Freiburg from 1991 to 2007, had differences with Samuel Eto'o during qualifying and there was speculation of unrest in the camp.

Booking their place at the 2014 finals would no doubt have lifted the mood in the squad. Finke must harness that spirit and get his big players firing in the same way Valeri Nepomniachi did in 1990.

Cameroon set a new record for an African side when they booked themselves a place at their seventh FIFA World Cup finals with a 4–1 victory over Tunisia.

The west Africans reached Brazil 2014 with five wins, two draws and a sole defeat in qualifying but they have been written off by former captain Patrick Mboma.

"I'm under no illusions and I don't expect us to do anything at the World Cup," said Mboma, who appeared at the 1998 and 2002 finals. "A surprise like we pulled off in 1990 won't be possible."

The former Paris Saint-Germain and Parma striker pointed to Cameroon's record since that tournament in Italy. They have reached four of the five subsequent showpiece events but have failed to make it past the group stage on each occasion, although they were continental champions in 2000 and 2002.

The current set of Cameroon players will be desperate to prove Mboma wrong. While a place in the last 16 would mark an improvement for the Indomitable Lions, captain Samuel Eto'o, who came out of international retirement ahead of the play-off against Tunisia, believes his team have the ability to reach the semi-finals.

"If we start preparing on time, we may not win the World Cup, but can do better than Ghana three years ago in South Africa," said

Left to right: Cameroon: (top row), Allan Nyom, Alex Song, Ndoubena Nkoulou, Aurelien Chedjou, Joel Matip, Charles Itandje, Samuel Eto'o; (bottom row) Dany Nounkeu, Pierre Webo, Enoh Eyong, Jean Makoun.

STAR MAN

SAMUEL ETO'O

(Samuel Eto'o Fils)
BORN: 10 March 1981
CLUB: Chelsea (England)

Samuel Eto'o has been a prolific goalscorer for both club and country. He has won league titles in Italy and Spain, as well as the UEFA Champions League three times. While the striker was also part of the Cameroon sides that won the CAF Africa Cup of Nations in 2000 and 2002, he is in danger of retiring without starring at a FIFA World Cup.

Eto'o has played in three previous finals – the first as a 17-year-old in 1998 – but has scored only three goals. Given the right service, the lethal marksman could bow out of international football on a high.

Cameroon's record goalscorer after qualifying for Brazil.

To go one better than their African rivals' quarter-final appearance, Cameroon need to improve dramatically on their performance at the same tournament. They left the 2010 FIFA World Cup without a single point after defeats to Japan, Denmark and the Netherlands.

They have since failed to reach the CAF Africa Cup of Nations in both 2012 and 2013, but those disappointments made the play-off victory all the sweeter for midfielder Jean Makoun, whose two second-half goals sealed his country's FIFA World Cup place.

"We've been through several long and difficult years," Makoun said. "Now, I think we have identified the problem, which is concord among us. We can achieve better results in the future and I think our performance shows that we have a bright future."

Cameroon appear determined to make up for past failures at this year's finals. They have the ability to shock a team or two, if they play to their strengths. Eto'o is Cameroon's marquee player and will be desperate to make the most of his last opportunity to make an impact on the world stage. The Chelsea striker dropped deep against Tunisia in a bid to give his team a creative spark but the Lions need him in the box, where he is at his most dangerous.

Cameroon have a strong and experienced defensive unit and should be difficult to break down. Stephane Mbia, Aurelien Chedjou, Alex Song and Makoun are all physical players and need to be at their best to lay a platform for Eto'o and his fellow attackers.

It will not be easy for Volker Finke's side in Brazil. The South American teams will be difficult to beat in their own backyard, while European heavyweights such as Germany, Spain and the Netherlands will have vastly superior squads.

To enjoy relative success at the 2014 FIFA World Cup, Cameroon will need to rekindle the spirit of 24 years ago. All eyes will be on Eto'o to see if he can follow Roger Milla's lead and deliver on the biggest stage of all in the twilight of his career.

Ghana stole Cameroon's thunder in South Africa. The Indomitable Lions will be determined to prove they are the best team in Africa and show they are not simply in Brazil to make up the numbers.

ONES TO WATCH

ALEX SONG

(Alexandre Dimitri Song Billong)
BORN: 9 September 1987
CLUB: Barcelona (Spain)

Alex Song is a midfield enforcer and will play a key role in protecting Cameroon's backline. He is strong in the tackle and comfortable on the ball. Song has plenty of UEFA Champions League experience and that will be crucial in the pressure-cooker environment in South America.

BENJAMIN MOUKANDJO

(Benjamin Moukandjo Bile)
BORN: 12 November 1988
CLUB: Nancy (France)

Benjamin Moukandjo was a slow starter at international level but there were signs in the play-off victory against Tunisia that he is warming to the task. The striker is quick, has a direct running style and is good with the ball at his feet, attributes which make him the perfect foil for the experienced Samuel Eto'o.

SPAIN

LA FURIA ROJA

FIFA WORLD CUP
Brasil

The FIFA World Cup holders head to Brazil bidding to become the first team to retain the trophy in 52 years. Vicente Del Bosque's men once more came through a qualification campaign unbeaten and will start the tournament among the favourites to reach the final at the Maracana.

COACH

VICENTE DEL BOSQUE

Vicente Del Bosque inherited a winning Spain team from Luis Aragones following UEFA EURO 2008 and few could have predicted how successful he would go on to be.

He is aiming to become only the second coach to win the FIFA World Cup twice after Vittorio Pozzo, who led Italy to their back-to-back successes in 1934 and 1938.

Before turning to international football, 63-year-old Del Bosque enjoyed a successful career at club level, winning the UEFA Champions League and La Liga each on two occasions with Real Madrid. He is the only manager to have won the Champions League, European Championship and FIFA World Cup.

History-makers Spain are looking to tear up the record books once again as they head to Brazil to defend the FIFA World Cup. By winning the UEFA European Championship in 2008 and 2012 either side of glory in South Africa in 2010, they became the only side to win three successive major international tournaments.

Now Vicente Del Bosque's men are aiming to become the first team to retain the FIFA World Cup since Brazil in 1962 and the only European winners on South American soil.

Such has been Spain's dominance on the international stage during their historic run, they have not conceded a single goal in the knockout phases of any of their three triumphs. They have lost only three competitive games since winning UEFA EURO 2008; their FIFA World Cup 2010 opener against Switzerland, a loss to the USA in the 2009 FIFA Confederations Cup semi-final, and last summer's final against Brazil in the 2013 competition.

Despite qualifying for the finals with an unbeaten record – as they did before South Africa in 2010 – and overcoming France in Paris, Spain received criticism during their campaign for a series of narrow wins against lower-ranked opposition. Head coach Del Bosque is confident his side will put on more of a show in Brazil.

"In the qualification group there have been four ugly, uncomfortable matches in which we haven't felt happy with the way we have played, but there were three where we played at a very good level,"

Left to right: Spain: (top row) Iker Casillas, Sergio Ramos, Sergio Busquets, Gerard Pique, Alvaro Negredo; (bottom row) Pedro Rodriguez, Jesus Navas, Alberto Moreno, Juan Francisco Torres, Andres Iniesta. Xavi Hernandez.

STAR MAN

ANDRES INIESTA

(Andres Iniesta Lujan)
BORN: 11 May 1984
CLUB: Barcelona (Spain)

The scorer of the winning goal in the 2010 FIFA World Cup final will once again be looked to for inspiration. The slight midfielder can play in the middle or from the left and offers a cutting edge to Spain's long spells of possession.

Andres Iniesta has received criticism for not scoring enough goals – he failed to score during the qualification campaign despite appearing in all eight games – but he showed in Johannesburg four years ago he can deliver at the crucial moments. His partnership with Xavi will once again be key.

SPAIN AT THE FIFA WORLD CUP™

1934	Quarter-finals
1950	4th place
1962	1st round
1966	1st round
1978	1st round
1982	2nd round
1986	Quarter-finals
1990	Round of 16
1994	Quarter-finals
1998	1st round
2002	Quarter-finals
2006	Round of 16
2010	CHAMPIONS

he said. "The opponents want to keep their dignity. In the World Cup it won't be like this because the possession will be shared more. The teams that have qualified are very strong and World Cups are a different thing. They are more open and fun."

On paper, Spain's side remains formidable. Captain Iker Casillas faces competition in goal from Victor Valdes and Pepe Reina, while Gerard Pique and Sergio Ramos form a fearsome defensive partnership. Jordi Alba was one of the breakthrough stars of UEFA EURO 2012 and offers penetration from left-back, though Del Bosque does not have the same sort of quality at right-back.

In midfield Spain possess an embarrassment of riches. Barcelona trio Xavi, Sergio Busquets and Andres Iniesta form the backbone of the team, with club team-mate Cesc Fabregas, Real Madrid's Xabi Alonso and Bayern Munich's Javi Martinez offering superb alternative options.

They do not enjoy the same luxury in attack though. Record goalscorer David Villa has found

himself out of favour in recent times, while Fernando Torres has struggled to hit the heights reached at UEFA EURO 2008.

English Premier League trio Alvaro Negredo, Michu and Roberto Soldado will compete for the right to lead the attack but Del Bosque – as he did at UEFA EURO 2012 – may choose to use David Silva or Fabregas as the furthest forward player, with Pedro Rodriguez or Jesus

Navas offering width on the right. There are also a host of talented youngsters coming through, with Asier Illarramendi and Isco hoping their first season at Real Madrid will be enough to earn a place, while former Spain U–21 captain Thiago Alcantara is also pushing for a place.

Whatever Del Bosque decides, they will start the tournament among the favourites. Written off before and during their last two major tournaments, Spain laughed off the criticism on their way to more silverware. This summer will be the ultimate test but should they hold aloft the trophy on 13 July, their status as one of the best sides in history will be confirmed.

ONES TO WATCH

PEDRO RODRIGUEZ

(Pedro Eliezer Rodriguez Ledesma)
BORN: 28 July 1987
CLUB: Barcelona (Spain)

Often overlooked by club and country for more high-profile team-mates, the winger performs a crucial role in attack. He hugs the right touchline to offer width and can burst into central areas to provide a finishing touch, as he showed during the 2011 UEFA Champions League final.

SERGIO RAMOS

(Sergio Ramos Garcia)
BORN: 30 March 1986
CLUB: Real Madrid (Spain)

Having appeared as a right-back in South Africa in 2010, Ramos has since transformed himself into one of the very best central defenders in world football. A rock at the back for club and country, he also offers a big threat from set-pieces, scoring two goals during Spain's qualifying campaign.

NETHERLANDS

THE ORANJE

The Netherlands are the FIFA World Cup's bridesmaid but never the bride, having reached three finals only to lose each one. There is always a weight of expectation surrounding a country with such footballing prestige and the current squad suggests they will again be a force.

COACH

LOUIS VAN GAAL

Louis van Gaal may have an uncompromising approach but a virtually unparalleled CV means he commands the respect he needs to be an effective coach at the highest level.

His managerial name was made at Ajax, whom he coached for six years in the 1990s and guided to back-to-back Champions League finals before spells with Barcelona, AZ Alkmaar and Bayern Munich. The national team called on him for a second time in July 2012, with Van Gaal dubbing it "the challenge which I've been waiting for".

In their iconic orange jerseys and playing their unique brand of 'total football', the Netherlands are always one of the most colourful and exciting teams at any FIFA World Cup.

The Dutch have constantly produced high-quality performers from Johan Cruyff, Ruud Krol and the two-time FIFA World Cup finalists in the 1970s, to Marco van Basten, Ruud Gullit and the side which won the 1988 UEFA European Championship, to Ajax's golden generation of Dennis Bergkamp, Marc Overmars and the De Boer twins, Ronald and Frank.

Today's team features players who in their own right belong alongside the great names in Dutch football history. Robin van Persie's goals led Manchester United to the 2012–13 English Premier League title, Arjen Robben struck the winner in the UEFA Champions League final later that season and in the 2010 FIFA World Cup, Wesley Sneijder scored five goals to help his side to the final.

In Brazil, the world will find out just how good this Netherlands team is. They breezed through qualifying to reach the 2010 FIFA World Cup in South Africa, winning all eight matches and conceding only twice, and they won nine out of 10 to qualify for UEFA Euro 2012.

There have been no bumps on the road to Rio either; the Netherlands were one of the first teams to book their spot in Brazil by winning seven of their first eight

Above: The Dutch team before an 8–1 qualifying thrashing of Hungary in Amsterdam.

STAR MAN

ROBIN VAN PERSIE

BORN: 6 August 1983
CLUB: Manchester United (England)

Robin van Persie's career always promised much and, after steering clear of any major injury in recent seasons, his world-class talent has truly shone through.

In recent campaigns he has been one of Europe's deadliest marksmen, grabbing the goals which clinched Manchester United's 20th domestic title in his first year at Old Trafford after moving from Arsenal.

The 30-year-old scored eight times in his country's first eight qualifiers too, and the newly-appointed skipper will be keen to produce on the greatest stage having struck just once in their run to the final in South Africa four years ago.

NETHERLANDS AT THE FIFA WORLD CUP™

1934	1st round
1938	1st round
1974	Runners-up
1978	Runners-up
1990	Round of 16
1994	Quarter-finals
1998	4th place
2006	Round of 16
2010	Runners-up

contests. Yet it can be difficult to determine which Netherlands team will turn up at major tournaments as they proved at UEFA Euro 2012, where they lost all three of their group games.

Under the management of current coach Louis van Gaal, back for a second stint with the Oranje, complacency will not be an issue at least. Van Gaal is one of Europe's most experienced tacticians, having presided over the rise of the all-conquering Ajax in the mid-90s before being handed the reins to other European giants such as Barcelona and Bayern Munich.

His previous time at the national team's helm ended poorly with the Netherlands missing out on a place at the 2002 FIFA World Cup in Japan and Korea, so there is a sense of unfinished business on Van Gaal's part.

"Van Gaal always has a clear idea of what he wants to achieve," said Van Persie. "I'm very happy about the way he's been managing the national team. He's very

straightforward and honest; it's a good strategy and he explains everything he does. I understand the choices he makes."

The Netherlands' hopes may well hinge on how the next generation fares when asked to complement their more experienced peers

under the world's spotlight. The back four in particular has a distinctively different look to the defence from four years ago which included veteran skipper Giovanni van Bronckhorst. Van Gaal has decided to blood PSV's Jetro Willems and Feyenoord duo Bruno Martins Indi and Stefan de Vrij – all three are in their early 20s.

That trio will be hoping to etch their names alongside the Dutch greats past and present. Going one further than those who finished runners-up in 1974, 1978 and 2010 will go some way to doing that.

ONES TO WATCH

ARJEN ROBBEN

BORN: 23 January 1984
CLUB: Bayern Munich (Germany)

The flying winger finally proved he could step up when required as he kept his cool to score the winning goal in the 2012 UEFA Champions League final.

It crowned a glorious treble for Bayern Munich and was just the latest medal for the former Chelsea and Real Madrid man. The 30-year-old possesses one of the sweetest left feet in the game and is just as effective as a provider or a goalscorer.

KEVIN STROOTMAN

BORN: 13 February 1990
CLUB: Roma (Italy)

Central midfielder Kevin Strootman is one of the main reasons behind the Netherlands' dominant displays in qualifying.

He mixes the ability to distribute the ball with a combative style to make him one of the world's most complete young midfielders and is a key bridge between his country's relatively inexperienced defence and an ageing group of attackers.

CHILE

LA ROJA

Having featured in the inaugural tournament and finished third as hosts in 1962, Chile will seek to further enhance a rich FIFA World Cup history after securing a ninth finals appearance by playing a free-flowing brand of football which is sure to attract support from many neutral fans.

COACH

JORGE SAMPAOLI

After his hopes of a professional playing career were dashed by injury as a teenager, Jorge Sampaoli turned his attention to coaching and gained plenty of experience in Peru before a successful stint in charge of Universidad de Chile.

Brought in to revive Chile's flagging fortunes after a run of defeats under Claudio Borghi, he immediately sought to rekindle the attacking philosophy of previous manager Marcelo Bielsa, with good effect.

Sampaoli's preference for a high-energy, pressing formation has allowed Chile to make the most of their gifted athletes, opening up teams with interchanging wide men, overlapping wing-backs and midfield runners from deep positions.

Chile earned plenty of plaudits for their performances at the FIFA World Cup finals four years ago with a promising young side and now look well-placed to fulfil their potential in Brazil.

Marcelo Bielsa helped mould several stars of the country's third-place finish at the 2007 FIFA U-20 World Cup into senior internationals ahead of the last tournament, with La Roja beating Honduras and Switzerland in the group stage. They lost nothing in defeat when going down 2-1 to Spain in their final pool match, before finding historic nemesis Brazil too strong in the round of 16.

Bielsa's departure was followed by a stagnant period under Claudio Borghi, but Jorge Sampaoli has restored an attacking philosophy and Chile will again be a team to watch after a strong finish in qualifying. Five wins and a 3-3 draw in Colombia from their last six matches helped La Roja to finish third in the South American pool, with only Argentina scoring more goals.

The development of star man Alexis Sanchez epitomises Chile's transition from a work in progress to a team of proven performers looking much more like the finished article.

Ahead of the 2010 FIFA World Cup finals in South Africa, he was regarded as a hot prospect who had just begun to make a serious impact for Udinese in Italy, but at the age of 21 he still had a lot of learning to do. The following season, Sanchez fired in a dozen Serie A goals and had 11 assists before being voted the world's most promising youngster prior to a big-money move to Barcelona.

Above: Chile line up before the qualifier against Bolivia in Santiago.

STAR MAN

ALEXIS SANCHEZ

(Alexis Alejandro Sanchez Sanchez)
BORN: 19 December 1988
CLUB: Barcelona (Spain)

Talent scouts have been tipping Alexis Sanchez as a potential superstar since a young age and he has not let them down, winning league titles in Chile with Colo-Colo, in Argentina with River Plate and in Spain with Barcelona, as well as shining for Udinese in Italy.

Sanchez uses speed and trickery to run at defenders and can play anywhere in the forward line, although his most impressive displays have come out wide, from where he can cut in and go for goal or set up others with his accurate and incisive passing.

After taking a little time to settle in at Camp Nou, he has won over the Catalan supporters with a series of crucial goals and exciting play to establish himself as one of the leading lights in La Liga and is perfectly placed to play a major role for Chile in Brazil.

Arturo Vidal is another who has raised his game to even higher levels in recent years, finding his niche as a box-to-box midfielder with Juventus – being dubbed 'the Warrior' by Italian journalists and winning a fans' player-of-the-year vote following their 2012–13 title triumph.

Vidal was Chile's joint top scorer with five goals alongside rising star Eduardo Vargas during their qualifying campaign, with Sanchez just one behind them – again highlighting how the key performers have now added greater consistency to their undoubted talent.

Other established senior players who have gained valuable experience at club level in major European leagues include Real Sociedad goalkeeper Claudio Bravo, Juventus wing-back

Mauricio Isla, Cardiff City enforcer Gary Medel and Fiorentina midfielder Matias Fernandez.

"There have been very good players that have emerged at various times in the past, but there have never been so many at the same time," said Vidal. "There are a number of us that are doing well both in Europe's major leagues and in the national team, which is something new for Chilean

football. It makes me proud to be part of this process."

Some sceptics will no doubt point an accusing finger at Chile's disappointing results away from home against other leading South American sides in qualifying, notably losing 4–1 in Argentina, 4–0 in Uruguay and 3–1 in Ecuador.

However, those setbacks occurred before Sampaoli turned things around, with Sanchez, Vidal and Vargas teaming up to score 12 of the 15 goals they netted between them throughout the whole of qualifying in the final six matches.

Add some impressive friendly results against the likes of Brazil and Spain, and Chile look ready, willing and able to do battle with any of the favourites for FIFA World Cup glory.

ONES TO WATCH

ARTURO VIDAL

(Arturo Erasmo Vidal Pardo)
BORN: 22 May 1987
CLUB: Juventus (Italy)

An emotional character whose desperate will to win led to some disciplinary problems early on in his career, Arturo Vidal has matured into an all-action midfield dynamo during spells with Bayer Leverkusen and Juventus. As well as being courageous and combative, he also has a creative spark when getting forward.

EDUARDO VARGAS

(Eduardo Jesus Vargas Rojas)
BORN: 20 November 1989
CLUB: Napoli (Italy)

After finishing second behind Neymar in the 2011 South American Player of the Year voting, Eduardo Vargas was signed by Napoli before being loaned out to Brazilian outfit Gremio. A graduate of the Universidad de Chile set-up which produced Marcelo Salas, he has a similarly natural talent when it comes to scoring goals.

AUSTRALIA

FIFA WORLD CUP
Brasil

THE SOCCEROOS

Australia have become an ever present at the FIFA World Cup finals in recent times as football has moved into a truly professional era Down Under. The Socceroos had reached the finals just once until 2006, but will be appearing for the third time in a row in Brazil.

Australia have established themselves as one of the heavyweights of Asian football since their move to that confederation in 2006, but they endured a nervous pathway to Brazil. The Socceroos had to wait until the dying moments of their final qualifier against Iraq to secure their passage, when striker Josh Kennedy headed the only goal of a 1–0 win in the 83rd minute.

The relief of a sport-loving nation, now starting to prove its football pedigree, was palpable as 80,500 fans celebrated wildly inside ANZ Stadium in Sydney.

"It's amazing for the country. That's three World Cups now," captain Lucas Neill said after the match. "Six months ago, it was looking a bit sticky but we have stuck together."

Australia's hopes had looked in grave danger following a shock loss in Jordan midway through qualifying as questions started to be asked of the ageing squad. Those same players had led Australia to the previous two FIFA World Cup finals as well as the final of the 2011 Asian Cup, when they lost to Japan in extra time.

Their experience finally shone through in the end as a battling 1–1 draw against Japan in Saitama was followed with home wins against Jordan and Iraq to secure qualification.

It was not enough for coach Holger Osieck to keep his job, though, as results began to go against him. Consecutive 6–0 defeats away to Brazil and France prompted Osieck's departure last October, with two-time A-League

COACH

ANGE POSTECOGLOU

The new Australia coach faces a tough task of balancing the old and the new after being handed the reins in October.

Holger Osieck guided the Socceroos to the finals, but consecutive 6–0 defeats to Brazil and France prompted his departure. Postecoglou must find a way to integrate younger players with the likes of Harry Kewell, Lucas Neill and Tim Cahill, yet still remain competitive at the 2014 FIFA World Cup. It is a task many Down Under believe he is capable of after nurturing Brisbane Roar into an unbeatable force en route to A-League titles in 2010–11 and 2011–12.

Above: The Socceroos line up before their victory over Iraq in Sydney which confirmed qualification for the 2014 FIFA World Cup.

STAR MAN

TIM CAHILL

BORN: 6 December 1979
CLUB: New York Red Bulls (USA)

Tim Cahill has been Australia's most reliable performer on the big stage ever since he announced himself with a late double strike against Japan to secure the Socceroos' first ever win at a FIFA World Cup finals in 2006.

He may lack the eye-catching skill of other forwards but is blessed with a sixth sense to be in the right place at the right time, coupled with an aerial ability to catch the world's best defenders off guard, to ensure he is a constant menace in the box.

A main road in Sydney was named the 'Tim Cahill Expressway' before Australia's final FIFA World Cup qualifier against Iraq, which the Socceroos won 1-0 to book their place in Brazil.

AUSTRALIA AT THE FIFA WORLD CUP™

1978	1st round
2006	Round of 16
2010	1st round

Vidosic, Jackson Irvine and Ryan McGowan represent the core of the next generation.

Adding those players to the likes of veterans such as Tim Cahill, Mark Bresciano and Harry Kewell – who have seen it all on the biggest stage – as well as Crystal Palace skipper Mile Jedinak and Postecoglou has the makings of a squad to worry the big teams.

Australia have, of course, done that before at recent FIFA World Cup finals after beating Croatia and Serbia, while they were only beaten in the round of 16 by eventual champions Italy at the 2006 FIFA World Cup due to an injury-time Francesco Totti penalty.

In a country where sporting exploits define the mood of the nation, the Socceroos – backed by a vocal travelling support – can be expected to give their all to progress in Brazil.

winner Ange Postecoglou drafted in on a five-year contract.

The length of that deal reflected Football Federation Australia's desire to give Postecoglou the time to turn around an ageing squad and integrate young players.

He lost his most experienced player on the eve of his first match in charge against Costa Rica, when Chelsea goalkeeper Mark Schwarzer announced his international retirement. Schwarzer left as his country's most capped player (109) and a veteran of two FIFA World Cup finals, as well as being a key part of their qualification campaign.

In his place young goalkeeper Mitch Langerak has been preferred – despite a jarring debut against France – and the young Borussia Dortmund goalkeeper reflects the new wave of Australian players who fans hope can make the step up as their 'Golden Generation' start to filter out of the team.

In Robbie Kruse (Bayer Leverkusen), Tom Rogic (Celtic)

and James Holland (Austria Vienna), the Socceroos have talented young players who have enjoyed life in Europe's Champions League in the past season, while Tommy Oar, Rhys Williams, Dario

ONES TO WATCH

MITCH LANGERAK

BORN: 22 August 1988
CLUB: Borussia Dortmund (Germany)

Mitch Langerak has big shoes to fill following the international retirement of Mark Schwarzer.

The Borussia Dortmund stopper made a chastening debut against France last October when Australia lost 6-0, prompting former coach Holger Osieck's exit. The 25-year-old is well regarded Down Under and at Dortmund, where he has proved he has the size, athleticism and mental strength to cope with the big games.

ROBBIE KRUSE

BORN: 5 October 1988
CLUB: Bayer Leverkusen (Germany)

In an ageing side, Robbie Kruse has established himself as the most promising of the new generation of Australian players.

Scruffy-haired and an awkward running style hide a sharp sense on the pitch which has seen him leave Bundesliga defenders in his wake since moving to Germany in 2011. Kruse can pick a pass too and, since his move from Fortuna Dusseldorf to Bayer Leverkusen, has started to improve his goalscoring record.

GROUP C

COLOMBIA

FIFA WORLD CUP Brasil

LOS CAFETEROS

After over a decade in the wilderness, Colombia have discovered a second golden generation of players to recapture their glory days of the 1990s, when they reached three straight FIFA World Cup finals, although Los Cafeteros will hope to hit the headlines for happier reasons this time.

Colombia's FIFA World Cup history will always be tinged with sadness following the murder of Andres Escobar after scoring an own goal in a shock loss to the USA at the 1994 finals but there is genuine hope of the current squad creating fonder memories in Brazil.

Los Cafeteros failed to qualify for the last three tournaments as they struggled to replace star performers such as Carlos Valderrama, Faustino Asprilla, Freddy Rincon and eccentric goalkeeper Rene Higuita.

However, with £50m Monaco striker Radamel Falcao leading the way up front and veteran captain Mario Yepes providing a steadying influence in defence, Colombia hit a rich vein of form which saw them finish second in the South America qualifying group and reach as high as third in the FIFA/Coca-Cola World Ranking at one point.

The potential was there for all to see at the 2011 Copa America when they claimed wins over Costa Rica and Bolivia and drew with hosts Argentina, all without conceding a single goal, to top their pool before frustratingly going out to Peru in extra time in the quarter-finals.

Jose Pekerman rallied his troops to secure an impressive nine wins and three draws from 16 games on the road to Rio, with notable results being a 4-0 thrashing of Uruguay and a 5-0 rout of Bolivia, as well as again holding Argentina to a goalless draw in Buenos Aires.

Los Cafeteros completed their best ever FIFA World Cup qualifying campaign when coming

COACH

JOSE PEKERMAN

After an uneventful playing career was cut short by a knee injury at the age of 28, Jose Pekerman established himself as an excellent coach of junior teams before taking charge of the Argentina youth set-up.

Three FIFA World Youth Championship triumphs at Under-20 level followed in 1995, 1997 and 2001 before he took over the senior side for the 2006 FIFA World Cup, where La Albicelestes impressed before losing out to hosts Germany on penalties.

Since switching to Colombia, Pekerman has never been afraid to experiment with different formations and often prefers to select players for a specific role above higher-profile squad members.

Left to right: Colombia: (top row) Mario Yepes, David Ospina, Carlos Sanchez, Abel Aguilar, Luis Perea; (bottom row) Teofilo Gutierrez, Macnelly Torres, Camilo Zuniga, Radamel Falcao, Juan Cuadrado, Pablo Armero.

STAR MAN

RADAMEL FALCAO
(Radamel Falcao Garcia Zarate)
BORN: 10 February 1986
CLUB: Monaco (France)

Radamel Falcao established himself as a rising star with River Plate in Argentina and flourished when he moved to Europe, where he helped both Porto and Atletico Madrid to claim Europa League triumphs, scoring 29 times during those two campaigns.

Falcao also hit a hat-trick for Atletico in a UEFA Super Cup defeat of Chelsea and led his side to a Copa del Rey victory when beating city rivals Real Madrid in the final.

Those exploits earned him a move to Monaco and after scoring nine goals for Colombia in their qualifying campaign, Falcao is rated one of the most clinical strikers on the planet.

a strong team and they've not just won games, they've done it by playing good football."

Valderrama is also a fan of Pekerman, adding: "He's a football man who can play the game and who, in his own way, has given Colombian football its identity back. The players have adapted to him and are getting the results that Colombia and the world like to see."

The fact that Pekerman will be able to call on players who have already proved themselves at the highest level in Spain, Italy, Germany, France, Netherlands and Portugal augurs well for an improved performance in their fifth FIFA World Cup finals.

Escobar famously wrote "life doesn't end here" in reaction to Colombia's early exit 20 years ago and his predecessors will be determined to honour his memory with impressive displays in Brazil.

from behind to win 2-1 in Paraguay, despite having Fredy Guarin sent off after 31 minutes, with Yepes proving an unlikely hero when adding to the solitary goal he had scored in 50 previous qualifiers by netting twice.

Colombia had earlier rallied from 3-0 down to draw with Chile in a game which guaranteed them a trip to the finals, while in friendlies they had drawn with Brazil in New York and shown impressive form against teams from other continents by beating both Cameroon and Serbia.

The great Colombia teams of the 1990s failed to shine on the biggest stage but Valderrama, the iconic talisman of that era, believes the current squad may be better equipped to hold their form thanks to the experience of playing in different countries at club level.

He said: "It's different because this whole group of players play outside Colombia. These players have been abroad a long time and that gives them a bit more

international experience, tasting a different culture and way of life. I think this generation has the edge on ours because of that. It's exciting because we've always had generations of very good players who've somehow got lost along the way. Now they've assembled

ONES TO WATCH

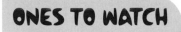

JAMES RODRIGUEZ
(James David Rodriguez Rubio)
BORN: 12 July 1991
CLUB: Monaco (France)

Due to his superb technical skills and balance, many have compared James Rodriguez to Colombia legend Carlos Valderrama, earning him the nickname El Neuvo Pibe (the new kid). He followed in the footsteps of Radamel Falcao when topping the scoring charts in Portugal with Porto before joining Monaco for a reported €45m.

FREDY GUARIN
(Fredy Alejandro Guarin Vasquez)
BORN: 30 June 1986
CLUB: Inter Milan (Italy)

Another creative playmaker in midfield, Fredy Guarin picked up three Portuguese titles and a host of other medals during his time with Porto before moving to Inter Milan. At San Siro, he has filled the void left by Dutch star Wesley Sneijder's departure and, as well as assisting others, is always capable of scoring crucial goals himself.

GREECE

TO PEIRATIKO

It is only 20 years since Greece first featured at the FIFA World Cup finals but they have made great progress as a footballing nation since. Having unexpectedly been crowned European champions in 2004, they will need no convincing they can once again upset some of the favourites.

COACH

FERNANDO SANTOS

Fernando Santos had enjoyed several managerial positions in Greek football with Panathinaikos (2001-02), AEK Athens (2004-06) and PAOK (2007-10) before taking charge of the national team after the 2010 FIFA World Cup.

In his playing days, Santos starred at left-back for his hometown club Benfica in Portugal before two-year spells with Maritimo and Estoril-Praia prior to his retirement in 1975.

After graduating with an electrical and telecomms engineering degree and pursuing a career as a technician, he returned to football in his first managerial role with Estoril Praia in 1987 before enjoying plenty of success in both Portugal and Greece.

A decade ago, Greece lifted the UEFA European Championship trophy at the Estadio da Luz after famously upsetting the odds to beat hosts Portugal in the final.

Four years later they climbed to their highest ever FIFA/Coca-Cola World Ranking of eighth, a feat which they achieved again in October 2011.

There has been much for Greece fans to celebrate in recent times, but they are yet to enjoy similar levels of success at the FIFA World Cup finals, where they have so far managed just a solitary victory.

They first qualified for the finals in 1994 but their performances in the United States proved to be a massive anti-climax: Having qualified with an unbeaten record, they were thrashed 4-0 by both Argentina and Bulgaria before a 2-0 loss to Nigeria saw them return home with no points and no goals.

Greece returned to the FIFA World Cup finals in South Africa in 2010 but, although they managed a first win against Nigeria, defeats to Korea Republic and Argentina again saw them eliminated at the group stage.

Fernando Santos' side will be out to make it third time lucky for Greece when they arrive in Brazil, or at least provide a better account of themselves. This is his first FIFA

Above: Greece line up before the vital play-off second leg against Romania.

STAR MAN

GEORGIOS KARAGOUNIS

BORN: 6 March 1977
CLUB: Fulham (England)

Captain Georgios Karagounis has been a familiar name on the Greece team sheet over the last 15 years and holds the all-time record for the most appearances for the national team.

After progressing through the age groups, he got his first call-up to the senior national side against El Salvador in 1999 and featured in the qualifying rounds of the 2002 FIFA World Cup for which Greece did not qualify.

He was a key player for Greece as they triumphed at UEFA EURO 2004, including memorably scoring the opening goal of the tournament.

World Cup tournament as manager of Greece after taking over from Otto Rehhagel following the 2010 showpiece.

The Portuguese coach led Greece to the play-offs in European qualifying where they beat Romania 4–2 over two legs to secure their trip to South America. It was a fitting reward for their performances in Group G after winning eight and losing just one of their qualifying games but agonisingly missing out on top position in the group to Bosnia-Herzegovina on goal difference.

Greece's European success in 2004 was based on a solid defence and that remains the case, having conceded only four goals in their 10 qualifying group games. Only Spain let in fewer goals in Europe and half of those 10 games were won by a 1–0 scoreline.

In goal, the reliable Orestis-Spyridon Karnezis was the only player to play every minute of the qualifying campaign. He is protected by a well-organised defence while the midfield is, as ever, likely to be marshalled

by veteran captain Georgios Karagounis at the age of 37.

Greece are undoubtedly renowned for their defensive nature and grit but they also have recognised names and prowess going forward.

Sotiris Ninis has risen through the international ranks and the pacy attacking midfielder will be hoping to make more of an impact

in Brazil after two substitute appearances in South Africa.

Celtic striker Georgios Samaras has featured in the past three major tournaments and also has plenty of UEFA Champions League experience, while the well-travelled Theofanis Gekas was top scorer in European qualifying for the 2010 finals and chipped in with two goals this time.

The main attacking threat in qualifying was Konstantinos Mitroglou, who netted five goals including three crucial strikes in the play-off against Romania. Greece will hope his ability to perform under pressure continues in Brazil as they aim to advance beyond the group stage for the first time.

ONES TO WATCH

KYRIAKOS PAPADOPOULOS

BORN: 23 February 1992
CLUB: Schalke 04 (Germany)

After making his professional debut at the age of 15, Kyriakos Papadopoulos has long since been attracting interest from some of Europe's biggest clubs and has become an established player for Schalke 04 following his move to the German Bundesliga in 2010.

He will still be only 22 in Brazil but has plenty of experience for a defender of his age.

SOTIRIS NINIS

BORN: 3 April 1990
CLUB: PAOK (Greece)

The midfielder can play both centrally or on the right and has been tipped to become a real attacking threat for Greece.

Sometimes referred to as their diamond in the rough, he has twice been voted as Greece's Footballer of the Year.

Injuries have affected his progress but now he will be hoping to seize the chance to shine in Brazil.

IVORY COAST

THE ELEPHANTS

Boasting by far the most talented group of players ever assembled by an African nation has not helped Ivory Coast to shine at the last two FIFA World Cup tournaments but hope springs eternal that they can show their true worth when it matters most in South America.

A golden generation of Ivory Coast players failed to live up to some high expectations in the last two FIFA World Cup finals but will be determined to make it third time lucky in Brazil.

The Elephants can call on star performers such as Didier Drogba, the Toure brothers Yaya and Kolo, Didier Zokora and Salomon Kalou, but have so far flattered to deceive in major tournaments.

Eight years ago in Germany, a 3–2 defeat of Serbia and Montenegro was not enough to repair the damage done by earlier losses to Argentina and the Netherlands as they trailed in a distant third in their group.

At South Africa 2010, Ivory Coast carried the hopes of the host continent but again came up short in a tough pool, drawing 0–0 with Portugal and losing 3–1 to Brazil before a 3–0 triumph over North Korea proved in vain.

The CAF Africa Cup of Nations has been another source of frustration, with Ivory Coast being favourites in the last five competitions but only managing to finish as runners-up in 2006 and 2012 in that time.

Nevertheless, they have rarely dropped out of the top 20 in the FIFA/Coca-Cola World Ranking in recent years and will hope the experience gained from those past disappointments can help them to at least reach the knockout stages this time around.

French coach Sabri Lamouchi has been charged with the task of succeeding where compatriot Henri Michel and Sweden's Sven-Goran Eriksson failed in past attempts and their qualifying campaign went smoothly enough. Four wins and two draws from

COACH

SABRI LAMOUCHI

The 42-year-old Sabri Lamouchi was a surprise choice to succeed Francois Zahoui as he had no previous coaching experience but time spent studying Jose Mourinho has helped him make the transition into management a smooth one.

A much-travelled midfielder during his playing days, he also clearly learned a lot from his time at clubs such as Inter Milan, Monaco and Marseille. Although picking up a dozen international caps for France, he just missed out on a place in their victorious 1998 FIFA World Cup squad, so will be keen to make his mark on the tournament as a manager.

Left to right: Ivory Coast: (top row) Yaya Toure, Kolo Toure, Sol Bamba, Romaric, Salomon Kalou; (bottom row) Jean-Jacques Gosso, Didier Zokora, Boubacar Barry, Didier Drogba, Serge Aurier, Gervinho.

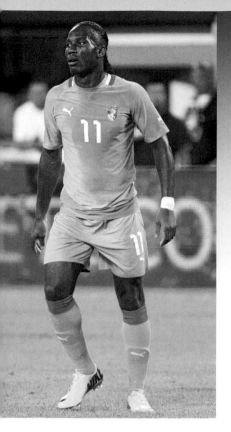

STAR MAN

DIDIER DROGBA

(Didier Yves Drogba Tebily)
BORN: 11 March 1978
CLUB: Galatasaray (Turkey)
Although now in his mid-30s, Didier Drogba remains Ivory Coast's talisman, leading from the front both on and off the field.

As well as scoring almost 250 goals for his country and top-class club sides such as Chelsea, Marseille and Galatasaray, he has twice been named African Footballer of the Year and throughout his incredible career has proved the man for the big occasion in many major matches.

Drogba signed off his eight-year stint at Chelsea with man-of-the-match displays in FA Cup and UEFA Champions League final wins and it would be fitting for him to finally shine on the biggest stage of all.

to be making footballing history in my country.

"We want to do something special at this World Cup. The last two have been difficult so we're hoping for a bit more luck this time around and we want to get through the first round at the very least."

Lamouchi has worked hard to both qualify for Brazil 2014 and build towards the future, giving greater responsibility to emerging stars such as Swansea striker Bony, Saint-Etienne midfielder Max Gradel and Anzhi Makhachkala forward Lacina Traore.

"Despite suffering at times over the last 18 months, I am extremely proud," said Lamouchi. "The players have worked hard and we've somehow managed to build something. Now we have to keep heading down this path."

Hopes are high that Ivory Coast can make a serious impact in Brazil and when it comes to learning the lessons of past mistakes, they do say elephants never forget!

six matches saw Ivory Coast comfortably top a group that also contained Morocco, Tanzania and Gambia, netting 15 goals and conceding only five as big guns Kalou, Yaya Toure and Drogba led the scoring alongside rising star Wilfried Bony.

The Elephants then beat 2002 FIFA World Cup quarter-finalists Senegal 4–2 on aggregate in the play-offs, with Kalou scoring in both a 3–1 home win over the Lions of Teranga and a 1–1 draw in Casablanca that booked their trip to Brazil.

"It hasn't been easy so far but when we all work for one another, we get our just rewards," said Lille forward Kalou, who previously shone with Chelsea and Feyenoord. "When things are tough, the important thing is to knuckle down. Football is a team game and all of the players deserve this reward."

Drogba is relishing the chance of one more crack at FIFA World Cup

glory following a glittering club career that has seen him pick up numerous honours with Marseille, Chelsea and Galatasaray.

"It's the third straight World Cup for a small country like ours," the powerful forward said. "I'm proud to be a part of this adventure and

ONES TO WATCH

YAYA TOURE

(Gnegneri Yaya Toure)
BORN: 13 May 1983
CLUB: Manchester City (England)
Moving from Barcelona to Manchester City allowed Yaya Toure to step out from the shadows of Lionel Messi, Andres Iniesta and Xavi and establish himself as a dominant midfield force in his own right. As well as being an immense physical presence, he also has superb shooting ability and can score spectacular long-range goals.

SERGE AURIER

BORN: 24 December 1992
CLUB: Toulouse (France)
After showing plenty of promise as a teenager at Lens, Serge Aurier has developed into an accomplished right-back at Toulouse, leading to transfer speculation linking him with several major European clubs, including Arsenal. Defensively sound, he also offers a genuine attacking threat on the overlap and adds youthful exuberance to an ageing side.

JAPAN

FIFA WORLD CUP
Brasil

BLUE SAMURAI

Japan had little trouble in qualifying for their fifth successive FIFA World Cup finals and, having twice reached the round of 16, hopes are now high that a talented squad can progress further than ever before in Brazil.

COACH

ALBERTO ZACCHERONI
The highly-experienced Alberto Zaccheroni began the 14th role of his long managerial career by leading Japan to the 2011 Asian Cup, having succeeded Takeshi Okada.

The Italian likes to play a 4–2–3–1 formation with a high defensive line and a quick passing style which he has quickly implemented in the Japanese set-up during his first role in international football.

After some morale-boosting friendly victories over the likes of Ghana, Korea Republic and Australia, the former AC Milan manager is setting his sights high in Brazil after a highly impressive qualifying campaign.

The first team to qualify for the 2014 FIFA World Cup finals, a new-look Japan side made easy work of reaching their fifth successive tournament.

The Asia Cup holders are blessed with a spine of talented individuals plying their trade in Europe, so could the next first-time winners of the trophy be Japan?

Boosted by a fourth-place finish at the London 2012 Olympics the Blue Samurai, reigning continental champions, look well-placed to improve on their penalty shoot-out elimination in the last 16 of the 2010 FIFA World Cup.

That exit at the hands of Paraguay came after Japan had surprised many by advancing from the group stage thanks to victories over Cameroon and Denmark and talk has now turned to a repeat display in Brazil. A quick look at their Asian qualifying campaign suggests that confidence is well placed. Alberto Zaccheroni's men averaged more than two goals a game and conceded only eight in 1,260 minutes of football to cruise through.

Their two-year journey to Brazil was not all plain sailing but early defeats to Uzbekistan and Korea DPR were soon forgotten as they began to gel and showed off their attacking flair.

They secured qualification in dramatic fashion, as Keisuke Honda's injury-time penalty earned them a 1–1 draw with Australia, an unassailable seven-point lead and

Left to right: Japan: (top row) Yasuhito Endo, Maya Yoshida, Yasuyuki Konno, Yoichiro Kakitani, Eiji Kawashima, Keisuke Honda; (bottom row) Makoto Hasebe, Atsuto Uchida, Yuto Nagatomo, Shinji Okazaki, Shinji Kagawa.

STAR MAN

KEISUKE HONDA

BORN: 13 June 1986
CLUB: AC Milan (Italy)

Playmaker Keisuke Honda has established himself as the Blue Samurai's talisman after stepping into the shoes of Hidetoshi Nakata and Shunsuke Nakamura.

Nicknamed 'Emperor Keisuke' for his stylish displays, Honda excelled during the 2010 FIFA World Cup with two goals and three man-of-the-match awards.

He is a versatile attacker and a dead-ball specialist who can play as a striker or on either wing, and it was his penalty against Australia which secured qualification.

The first Japanese footballer to play in the knockout stages of the UEFA Champions League, he had a goal-laden 2013 for his country.

JAPAN AT THE FIFA WORLD CUP™

1998	1st round
2002	Round of 16
2006	1st round
2010	Round of 16

established household names in European football and their regular exposure to top-level competition can only help their country's prospects.

Those star names are complemented by the likes of Standard Liege goalkeeper Eiji Kawashima, Southampton defender Maya Yoshida and the experienced cult hero Yasuhito Endo, who is now Japan's most capped player of all time.

Off the field, manager Zaccheroni and his all-Italian coaching staff bring their own decades of experience of Serie A football to the table, while radical changes to how youngsters are developed continue to pay dividends with the ultimate goal of making Japan a world-class football nation.

If Asia's top team live up to their undoubted potential at the FIFA World Cup in Brazil then this ambitious nation will move a step closer to doing just that.

sparked wild celebrations. Those scenes are something Zaccheroni is confident he will see again.

"Just qualifying is not enough," he said. "We will aim even higher in Brazil. I came to bring them to the World Cup – that was my bottom line. I feel relieved that I achieved it. We have a very strong commitment to playing well. We are going to improve further and surprise the world."

With 69,806 Japanese requests for tickets during the first phase of sales alone, they will certainly be backed by significant numbers and many have pointed to the thrilling attacking display in their 4–3 FIFA Confederations Cup defeat to Italy last summer as an example of what the travelling support can expect to see on the biggest stage.

While back at home the open and competitive J-League continues to blood home-grown talent, more than half of Zaccheroni's 23-man squad are with clubs in Europe, particularly the German Bundesliga.

Shinji Okazaki led the goalscoring charts during

qualification and the Mainz striker, who averages a goal every two games for his country, is joined in Germany by a number of his international colleagues including captain Makoto Hasebe (Nuremberg), right-back Atsuto Uchida (Schalke 04) and Hertha Berlin midfielder Hajime Hosogai.

Shinji Kagawa, Yuto Nagatomo and Keisuke Honda are all

ONES TO WATCH

SHINJI KAGAWA

BORN: 17 March 1989
CLUB: Manchester Utd (England)

An agile and technically gifted player with an eye for goal, Shinji Kagawa became the first Japanese player to play for Manchester United and won the league title in his maiden season after back-to-back titles with Borussia Dortmund in Germany.

The Asian International Footballer of the Year in 2012, he averages a goal every three games for his country.

YUTO NAGATOMO

BORN: 12 September 1986
CLUB: Inter Milan (Italy)

Since his international debut in 2008, full-back Yuto Nagatomo has been a crucial cog in the Japan side, earning more than 60 caps.

His eye-catching displays at the 2010 FIFA World Cup saw him named in Arsenal manager Arsene Wenger's team of the tournament. The 27-year-old is equally adept at full-back or on the left of midfield.

URUGUAY

LA CELESTE

Uruguay will forever be known as the nation that won the inaugural FIFA World Cup in 1930. They repeated the feat in Brazil 20 years later and have since made three semi-final appearances. The last of those came in 2010, which will give Uruguay heart going into a tournament closer to home.

Uruguay have become used to qualifying for the FIFA World Cup the hard way. For the fourth South American qualification campaign in a row, La Celeste finished fifth, meaning they faced another intercontinental play-off. Jordan were the opponents on this occasion and they were blown away in the first leg in Amman. The 5–0 victory showed just how dangerous this Uruguay team is when it really matters, before they played out a goalless draw in the return leg in Montevideo to seal qualification.

"We're all happy because the truth is it's been a hard road," said striker Edinson Cavani, who scored six goals in qualifying.

Oscar Tabarez's team have history on their side heading into the 2014 FIFA World Cup finals. Uruguay won the only other tournament staged in Brazil in 1950, beating the hosts in the deciding match of the four-team final group.

Tabarez will sense an opportunity in the first FIFA World Cup in Latin America since 1986. Uruguay will feel more at home in Brazil, which gives them an advantage over European heavyweights such as Spain and Germany.

The South Americans were also given a taste of what they might expect in Brazil at the FIFA Confederations Cup 2013 when they reached the semi-finals before losing to the hosts and eventual champions.

Tabarez was encouraged by his side's performance in that 2–1 defeat, in which Diego Forlan missed a first-half penalty before

COACH

OSCAR TABAREZ

'El Maestro', in his second spell as Uruguay coach, is regarded as one of the most astute coaches in world football. He is not afraid to make personnel changes and switch tactics to adapt to the opposition.

Oscar Tabarez's method has paid off. He led his country to the last 16 of the 1990 FIFA World Cup before taking the manager's job again in 2006.

During his second reign, Uruguay have finished fourth at three major tournaments and won another. La Celeste are in good hands under an experienced coach who knows a thing or two about tournament football.

Left to right: Uruguay: (top row) Edinson Cavani, Fernando Muslera, Christian Stuani, Diego Lugano, Luis Suarez, Diego Godin; (bottom row) Diego Perez, Egidio Arevalo, Maximiliano Pereira, Jorge Fucile, Cristian Rodriguez.

STAR MAN

LUIS SUAREZ
(Luis Alberto Suarez Diaz)
BORN: 24 January 1987
CLUB: Liverpool (England)
There is rarely a dull moment when Luis Suarez is around. The former Ajax striker is always in the game and although he sometimes makes the headlines for the wrong reasons, there is no doubting he is a quality player.

Give Suarez a chance in the box and he will invariably put it away. He netted three times at the last FIFA World Cup finals, was crowned the best player at the Copa America 2011 and scored 11 goals in qualifying.

Suarez's infamous handball in the quarter-final against Ghana in South Africa overshadowed his performances in that tournament and he will hope to let his feet do the talking in Brazil.

Paulinho grabbed a late winner for the Brazilians.

"I'm going away a proud man because I know that if we can play like that, we can give anyone a game," said Tabarez.

Uruguay certainly proved they have no reason to fear anyone at the 2010 FIFA World Cup finals in South Africa. They topped a group containing the host nation, France and Mexico before beating Korea Republic and Ghana on their way to the last four, where they lost 3–2 to the Netherlands in a thriller in Cape Town.

The main players in that run to the semi-finals are still around and will be better for the experience. In Luis Suarez and Cavani, Uruguay will have one of the best strikeforces at the tournament while the experienced Forlan, who won the adidas Golden Ball in South Africa, offers Tabarez another excellent option. Diego Godin is an important player in defence, with Maximiliano Pereira and Egidio Arevalo also key men.

As well as semi-final appearances at the 2010 FIFA World Cup and FIFA Confederations Cup 2013, the current crop of players won the Copa America 2011, so experience of the big occasions is certainly not a problem.

Tabarez's side may not be among the favourites to win the FIFA World Cup at the Maracana on

13 July but nations that write them off do so at their own peril.

Uruguay are a dangerous team, particularly in familiar surroundings, and if Suarez and Cavani click, there is a good chance *La Celeste* will enjoy another successful tournament.

"Our mindset is not to believe that the future is mapped out beforehand," said Tabarez following his team's 3–2 victory over Argentina in their final South American qualifier last October.

Uruguay believe their destiny is in their own hands and that is a good mindset to have. With the conditions in their favour, Uruguay may never get a better opportunity to be crowned world champions for a third time.

ONES TO WATCH

EDINSON CAVANI
(Edinson Roberto Cavani Gomez)
BORN: 14 February 1987
CLUB: Paris Saint-Germain (France)
Edinson Cavani was one of the hottest properties in world football before he moved from Napoli to Paris Saint-Germain for a Ligue 1 record fee. The forward has pace, skill and can score with both feet. His partnership with Luis Suarez has the ability to light up the tournament.

DIEGO GODIN
(Diego Roberto Godin Leal)
BORN: 16 February 1986
CLUB: Atletico Madrid (Spain)
Uruguay must make sure they are solid at the back to lay a platform for their lethal frontmen. Quick, powerful and composed, Diego Godin is central to La Celeste's hopes of shutting out the world's best strikers. He could be as important to Uruguay as Luis Suarez and Edinson Cavani.

COSTA RICA

LOS TICOS

Costa Rica missed out on reaching the 2010 FIFA World Cup finals by the tightest of margins but Jorge Luis Pinto's reinvigorated side are back at the greatest show on earth in 2014 after booking their place in Brazil with two qualifying matches to spare.

COACH

JORGE LUIS PINTO

Jorge Luis Pinto dreamed of taking Costa Rica to the FIFA World Cup when he first took charge of Los Ticos in 2004.

A disappointing run of results led to his dismissal in 2005 and Pinto's hopes of managing at the world's greatest football competition looked doomed.

Following an unsuccessful spell with his native Colombia, Pinto returned for a second stint as Costa Rica boss in 2011 and this time his dream has become reality.

Pinto guided the team to victory at the 2013 Copa Centroamericana before securing qualification for Brazil with two games to play.

Central American champions Costa Rica head to their fourth FIFA World Cup finals looking to show how far they have come since their disappointing showing in the 2006 competition.

Los Ticos failed to pick up a single point as they finished bottom of their group in Germany, but a lot has changed since then.

Former greats such as Paulo Wanchope, Walter Centeno and Rolando Fonseca have made way for a new generation of talented players who, under the stewardship of coach Jorge Luis Pinto, have the potential to go further than any Costa Rica side has gone in this competition. More of Costa Rica's players are plying their trade in Europe than ever before and this has given a huge boost to the national side. Fulham striker Bryan Ruiz, Levante shot-stopper Keylor Navas and Arsenal forward Joel Campbell were among the 12 European-based players in Costa Rica's squad for the final round of qualifying matches.

With so many members of their first team facing world-class internationals on a weekly basis, Los Ticos are a much stronger outfit now than they have been in the past.

Costa Rica competed at their

Above: Costa Rica line up before the qualifying match against USA in San Jose in September.

STAR MAN

BRYAN RUIZ
(Bryan Jafet Ruiz Gonzalez)
BORN: 18 August 1985
CLUB: Fulham (England)
Seen by many as Costa Rica's most exciting export, Fulham playmaker Bryan Ruiz is a tall yet technical number 10 who poses a serious attacking threat both in the air and on the floor.

The striker's close control, relentless desire to take players on and phenomenal ability to head the ball make him a real handful for defenders.

The former FC Twente striker has never been to the FIFA World Cup finals before and he will be looking to make a big impression when he leads his country out on the biggest stage of all, with the opportunity to show his sublime skills to the world.

first FIFA World Cup in 1990, when victories over Sweden and Scotland in the group stage saw them reach the last 16 – the furthest they have gone in the competition to date.

They were unable to build on their success in Italy, failing to qualify for the finals in the USA in 1994 and France in 1998.

Confidence was high in the build-up to the 2002 FIFA World Cup after they finished first in the qualifying table, six points ahead of the chasing pack, but a heavy defeat to Brazil in the final group game saw them miss out on making the last 16 only on goal difference.

Los Ticos also qualified for the 2006 FIFA World Cup in Germany but did not give a very good account of themselves, losing all three of their group games in what was a tournament to forget for fans and players alike.

Costa Rica lost to Uruguay in a 2010 qualification play-off, denying them the chance to play at their

third successive tournament but they are back this year and, some would argue, look better than ever.

Colombian coach Pinto is the man who has been charged with the task of leading this group of talented youngsters. The vast majority of his players have not been to a FIFA World Cup finals

before but they are not the only ones.

Pinto has yet to take a team to the most prestigious competition in football and he is incredibly excited about the prospect of managing at his first ever FIFA World Cup – so much so that he broke down in tears during an interview with Costa Rican radio station Columbia on the night that his side qualified for the tournament.

He said: "I've worked all my life, so hard, to make it to the World Cup, all my life; this is sheer happiness."

With such a passionate manager at the helm and a group of players growing in experience, confidence and ability, Costa Rica have the potential to make a real splash in Brazil.

ONES TO WATCH

ALVARO SABORIO
(Alvaro Alberto Saborio Chacon)
BORN: 25 March 1982
CLUB: Real Salt Lake (USA)
Alvaro Saborio is a strong forward with a tremendous goalscoring record for both club and country.

He is Real Salt Lake's all-time leading marksman, and was comfortably Costa Rica's highest scorer in qualifying. He spent much of the 2006 FIFA World Cup campaign on the bench.

JOEL CAMPBELL
BORN: 26 June 1992
CLUB: Arsenal (England)
Arsenal youngster Joel Campbell is a lightning-quick, attack-minded forward with a trick up his sleeve and an eye for goal.

Campbell has developed his game during successful loan spells with Lorient, Real Betis and Olympiacos since joining Arsene Wenger's club from Costa Rican outfit Deportivo Saprissa in 2011.

ENGLAND

THE THREE LIONS

A football-mad nation which played a pivotal role in forming the sport has been hoping for a repeat of its FIFA World Cup triumph in 1966 for almost half a century. Several heartaches may have curbed those expectations but England are always fancied to do well.

COACH

ROY HODGSON

The vastly-experienced 66-year-old, whose extensive coaching career began in Sweden, is no stranger to the international set-up and his time with Switzerland, the United Arab Emirates and Finland made him the ideal candidate when the Football Association needed a replacement for Fabio Capello in May 2012.

An affable manager, he was also handed the reins at club level in Denmark, Italy and his native England before his current position, which he inherited just months before being thrust in at the deep end at UEFA EURO 2012. England did not lose a game in normal time at that tournament, eventually going out to Italy on penalties and, after another two years to shape the team in his style, Roy Hodgson will be seeking an improvement in South America.

Since Bobby Moore famously lifted the Jules Rimet Trophy on home soil at Wembley, the Three Lions have continued to fall just short at FIFA World Cup finals thanks to some of the tournament's most iconic moments. There was Diego Maradona's 'Hand of God' goal for Argentina in 1986, Paul Gascoigne's tears in Italy four years later and David Beckham's petulant red card in 1998.

At the 2010 FIFA World Cup, though, England could not really point to a single pivotal reason as they were swept aside by an energetic, fresh Germany side 4–1 in the Round of 16 in South Africa. With Holland and Spain eventually contesting the final that year, English football was forced to reconsider its place among Europe's elite.

The perplexing thing, the critics said, was why those players at huge clubs such as Manchester United, Chelsea and Arsenal – all frequently successful on the continent – did not appear to be translating their form to the international arena.

Under current coach Roy Hodgson, however, faith has slowly but surely begun to be restored. England may not have booked their spot at the 2014 FIFA World Cup finals until the last round of qualifying matches but

Left to right: England: (top row) Kyle Walker, Rickie Lambert, Phil Jagielka, Joe Hart, Gary Cahill, Frank Lampard; (bottom row) Theo Walcott, James Milner, Steven Gerrard, Ashley Cole, Jack Wilshere.

STAR MAN

STEVEN GERRARD

BORN: 30 May 1980
CLUB: Liverpool (England)

The English love a leader and captain Steven Gerrard will hope to galvanise his team-mates at the 2014 FIFA World Cup finals with the type of driving runs which have been the hallmark of his career for club and country.

An energetic, all-action central midfielder able to make long-range passes, Gerrard still has the knack of bursting into the area and scoring crucial goals, as he proved with the one which sealed England's qualification in the 2-0 win against Poland.

The Liverpool man is probably entering his final major international tournament as a player but is still good enough to affect games, particularly with his deadly set-piece deliveries.

ENGLAND AT THE FIFA WORLD CUP™

1950	1st round
1954	Quarter-finals
1958	1st round
1962	Quarter-finals
1966	CHAMPIONS
1970	Quarter-finals
1982	2nd round
1986	Quarter-finals
1990	4th place
1998	Round of 16
2002	Quarter-finals
2006	Quarter-finals
2010	Round of 16

they did so without losing a game in Group H, scoring 31 goals and conceding only four in the process.

Captain Steven Gerrard and striker Wayne Rooney were in excellent form and the next generation, such as Arsenal's Jack Wilshere, Manchester United's Danny Welbeck and Tottenham's Andros Townsend, have provided more optimism.

Attacking football has not always been the English's forte but Hodgson's team has been involved in the occasional thriller under his guidance too – an exciting 2-2 draw with Brazil at the Maracana Stadium in June last year was testament to that.

"I have great trust in my players that they will not let us down," said Hodgson of England's chances in Brazil after qualification was secured. "We've been working together for 18 months and the way we play has changed. We're getting better all the time and hopefully will get better still. The

players really are a group and they trust each other."

After years of so-called underachievement, there is a theory that flying under the radar will suit England more. Gerrard is happy to run with that idea, insisting they have the potential to surprise their critics. "What is important is we have shown

everyone we are a good team," said the Liverpool midfielder. "We have not felt sorry for ourselves when we have had criticism, we have rolled our sleeves up, tried to work hard and put it right.

"It is a great feeling to be in Brazil and hopefully we can go in with a little less pressure on ourselves and surprise a few."

Likely to be backed as ever by a huge travelling support yearning for a return to those glory days of Moore, Alf Ramsey and Geoff Hurst, it will not take much for a nation to start dreaming and believing again.

ONES TO WATCH

WAYNE ROONEY

BORN: 24 October 1985
CLUB: Manchester Utd (England)

A mainstay in the England set-up since he burst on to the scene as a raw teenager, the always-willing Wayne Rooney possesses an abundance of pace and power.

The Manchester United forward has intelligence too and will be relied upon for his guile in England's attack.

JACK WILSHERE

BORN: 1 January 1992
CLUB: Arsenal (England)

The 22-year-old is expected to be a key member of England's midfield for years to come, having first been included in the squad in August 2010. Injuries have held him back since then but he highlighted his ability with a man-of-the-match performance in the 2-1 victory over Brazil at Wembley last year.

GROUP D

ITALY

THE AZZURRI

Italy head to Brazil with an excellent chance of becoming the first European nation to lift the FIFA World Cup trophy in South America. The Azzurri reached the 2012 UEFA European Championship final and claimed third place at the 2013 FIFA Confederations Cup.

Italy may have hit rock bottom in South Africa but Cesare Prandelli's men are firmly in the ascendancy and confidently targeting a fifth FIFA World Cup victory at the 2014 finals in Brazil.

Marcello Lippi guided the Azzurri to glory in Germany but could not repeat the feat four years later in South Africa, when Italy failed to win a single group game and left the tournament two weeks early without their precious trophy.

A change was needed and experienced Serie A coach Prandelli was quickly lured from Fiorentina, the club he had steered into the last 16 of the UEFA Champions League earlier in 2010.

Italy soon topped their qualification group to reach the 2012 UEFA European Championship and three goals from Prandelli's protégé Mario Balotelli helped them reach the final. World champions Spain may have proved too strong for the Italians in Kiev but a reinvigorated and exciting young team was starting to emerge under Prandelli's supervision.

A third-placed finish at the 2013 FIFA Confederations Cup then punctuated a near-flawless FIFA World Cup qualifying campaign that saw Italy become one of the first nations to book their tickets to Brazil.

Concerns remain over a lack of star power so one man Prandelli is desperate to see board the plane is Balotelli. The eccentric AC Milan striker has struggled with disciplinary issues on and off the pitch but can win games on his own when the mood

COACH

CESARE PRANDELLI

Italy needed a change of direction after a disappointing experience at the 2010 FIFA World Cup. Cesare Prandelli had done a fine job of reviving Fiorentina's fortunes and quickly restored pride and fighting spirit in the Italy camp.

Inside two years, he guided the team to the final of the 2012 UEFA European Championship – where they were only beaten by world champions Spain – and to qualification for the 2014 FIFA World Cup finals with two matches to spare for the first time in Italy's history.

Prandelli plans to return to club management on his return from Brazil but he will be determined to end on a high.

Above: Italy line up before their qualifying match against Denmark in Copenhagen in October.

STAR MAN

MARIO BALOTELLI

(Mario Barwuah Balotelli)
BORN: 12 August 1990
CLUB: AC Milan (Italy)

Unpredictable, temperamental but undeniably talented, the mood in which Mario Balotelli arrives in Brazil could be key for Italy.

The mercurial striker was on Manchester City's books when his three goals helped the Azzurri reach the final of the 2012 UEFA European Championship but since returning to Italy with AC Milan, he has truly blossomed. Fantastic ball control and deadly aim make him unstoppable on his day and until September 2013 he boasted a 100 per cent success rate from the penalty spot.

ITALY AT THE FIFA WORLD CUP™

1934	CHAMPIONS
1938	CHAMPIONS
1950	1st round
1954	1st round
1962	1st round
1966	1st round
1970	Runners-up
1974	1st round
1978	4th place
1982	CHAMPIONS
1986	Round of 16
1990	3rd place
1994	Runners-up
1998	Quarter-finals
2002	Round of 16
2006	CHAMPIONS
2010	1st round

takes him. Balotelli boasts the combined talents of every type of forward and is just as comfortable dribbling from deep to finish with finesse as he is when steering home an unstoppable free-kick or converting a penalty under intense pressure.

"Is it possible to go to the World Cup without him? Absolutely not," Prandelli said.

"I'm convinced that Mario won't do anything out of the ordinary again and that he'll arrive at the World Cup well prepared.

"I spoke to him and he said that was his dream. He needs to leave his problems behind and stop being the character that he's become."

Prandelli has successfully blended youth into his experienced squad, blooding exciting talents such as Marco Verratti, Stephan El Shaarawy and Lorenzo Insigne alongside FIFA World Cup winners Andrea Pirlo and Gianluigi Buffon, who is Italy's most-capped player.

Italy's traditional strength has always been in defence, where Giorgio Chiellini, Andrea Barzagli and Leonardo Bonucci are rated among the toughest centre-backs

in world football. The versatility offered by wide players Christian Maggio, Alessio Cerci and Stephan El Shaarawy means Italy's rivals can never be sure what to expect and, furthermore, the Azzurri have already proved they can match holders Spain.

They nullified La Roja's fearsome attacking threat in a goalless draw at the 2013 FIFA Confederations Cup, in which they also gave host

nation Brazil a scare, and they dominated fellow FIFA World Cup hopefuls Germany when they met at the 2012 UEFA European Championship.

Italy may well have to tackle either of those European giants, or hosts Brazil, if they are to be crowned world champions once more and the luxury of meeting all three in recent competitive games is one that few other nations have enjoyed.

ONES TO WATCH

LORENZO INSIGNE

BORN: 4 June 1991
CLUB: Napoli (Italy)

The young Napoli striker has already impressed with the senior team, but it was his match-winning free-kick against England at the 2013 UEFA U-21 European Championship that really captured the imagination of Italy fans.

Also in his element when creating plays around the penalty area, Lorenzo Insigne could be a surprise package in Brazil.

MARCO VERRATTI

BORN: 5 November 1992
CLUB: Paris Saint-Germain (France)

Brazil may prove to be the last FIFA World Cup destination for veteran Italy playmaker Andrea Pirlo but relative newcomer Marco Verratti has many years at the top ahead of him.

The pass-master from Pescara was fast-tracked through the U-21 set-up, made his senior debut against England in August 2012 and scored his first goal against Holland in February 2013.

SWITZERLAND

LA NATI

After failing to make the last 16 in South Africa four years ago, Switzerland issued a statement of intent by going unbeaten in their qualifying group. La Nati will be hoping to maintain their magnificent run of form when they head to their 10th FIFA World Cup finals.

COACH

OTTMAR HITZFELD

Ottmar Hitzfeld will be dreaming of adding one more trophy to his cabinet before bringing his managerial career to a close.

The former Germany international won almost everything there is to win in club football during spells with Borussia Dortmund and Bayern Munich, but has yet to win silverware since switching to international management in 2008. Hitzfeld masterminded the win which brought Spain's run of 11 straight victories to an end when they defeated the eventual champions in their opening game in South Africa four years ago, but they could not build on the result and were eliminated in the first round.

Hitzfeld announced in October that he will retire from management when the 2014 FIFA World Cup is over, describing it as "the most difficult decision" of his career.

Finishing Group E as runaway winners with 24 points from a possible 30, Switzerland were the surprise package in the qualification phase. Their impressive string of results saw them leap from 14th place to seventh in the October 2013 FIFA/Coca-Cola World Ranking, putting them among the top seeds for the showpiece in Brazil.

It is hard to believe this is the same national side that fell at the first hurdle in 2010 and failed to qualify for UEFA EURO 2012, but under the stewardship of one of the most successful coaches in football, Switzerland now boast a side capable of giving any team a run for their money.

With promising youngsters such as Bayern Munich playmaker Xherdan Shaqiri and experienced internationals like Stephan Lichtsteiner in their ranks, Switzerland have a talented, balanced squad ready to do battle in Brazil.

Coach Ottmar Hitzfeld believes being one of the top seeds will provide a major boost for his players.

"This status will make my players mentally even stronger," he told FIFA.com. "But I want them to keep their feet on the ground."

Although they have appeared in nine of the 19 FIFA World Cup competitions, Switzerland have never been past the quarter-finals stage. Many believe they have the potential to go far this time, and with their coach set to retire from football when the tournament is over, the players will be more motivated than ever.

Hitzfeld, who guided both Borussia Dortmund and Bayern Munich to UEFA Champions League glory before taking the reins at international level, has

Above: The Swiss team lines up before a 2013 friendly international against Greece in Athens.

STAR MAN

XHERDAN SHAQIRI

BORN: 10 October 1991
CLUB: Bayern Munich (Germany)
Pace, power and precision are just some of the attributes that make Bayern Munich midfielder Xherdan Shaqiri one of the brightest young players around. With his incredible ability to dribble past players and link up play, the 22-year-old is nothing short of deadly with the ball at his feet.

The 2012–13 UEFA Champions League winner may not be prolific in front of goal, but his propensity to create chances from nothing makes him a valuable asset to any team. Although he was included in Ottmar Hitzfeld's squad four years ago, Shaqiri made only one short substitute appearance and will be hoping to have more of an opportunity to show the world what he can do this time around.

overseen a steady improvement since his appointment in 2008.

Switzerland finished top of their group in Hitzfeld's first qualification campaign and then famously beat eventual winners Spain in their opening match at the 2010 FIFA World Cup finals, although they failed to progress beyond the first round.

After yet another successful qualifying stage, the former FC Basel striker announced that he will leave his role after the 2014 FIFA World Cup and Hitzfeld is hopeful of taking his side to new heights when he leads them out at the greatest show on earth for the second and final time.

He told FIFA.com: "Our goal in Brazil is to clear the group stage and keep going with as many matches as possible. There's no point in going to Brazil to play just three matches."

Despite powering their way through Group E, one thing that Switzerland did lack in qualifying

was an out-and-out goalscorer.

FC Basel defender Fabian Schaer was the leading scorer with three goals to his name, while forwards Mario Gavranovic (two) and Haris Seferovic (one) notched just three goals between them.

Hitzfeld will be looking for a bigger contribution from his strikers but has back-up in the form of goal-scoring midfielders, such as Gokhan Inler and Granit Xhaka, should his forwards fail to step up to the plate. Switzerland head into the tournament full of confidence and if this young team can fulfil their potential, the 2014 FIFA World Cup will be one to remember for Hitzfeld.

ONES TO WATCH

GRANIT XHAKA

BORN: 27 September 1992
CLUB: Borussia Moenchengladbach (Germany)
Borussia Moenchengladbach's Granit Xhaka is a tough-tackling midfielder who is one of the best around when it comes to turning defence into attack. The highly-rated 21-year-old has gone from strength to strength since moving to the Bundesliga from FC Basel in 2012 and will be looking to announce himself on the world stage when he heads to his first FIFA World Cup finals.

GOKHAN INLER

BORN: 27 June 1984
CLUB: Napoli (Italy)
Switzerland captain Gokhan Inler is attack-minded, strong and capable of scoring fantastic goals but probably the most valuable thing he brings to the team is his experience. The Napoli midfielder is one of the few Switzerland players who knows what it is like to play at a FIFA World Cup finals and he will play a vital part in preparing his younger team-mates for what lies ahead.

ECUADOR

LA TRICOLOR

Ecuador triumphed over adversity when reaching their third FIFA World Cup finals despite the tragic loss of one of their star players at a crucial point in the South American qualifying campaign, and will again be a highly-motivated band of brothers when the finals begin.

Ecuador showed an incredible strength of character to overcome the death of striker Cristian Benitez during their FIFA World Cup qualifying campaign and will be spurred on by the thought of further honouring his memory with a spirited showing in Brazil.

Benitez, affectionately known as Chucho to his friends and fans, had scored four goals for La Tricolor on the road to Rio before sadly passing away due to heart failure shortly after joining Qatar club El Jaish last summer.

The 58-times capped forward, who had previously enjoyed a stellar club career in his home country and Mexico, was just 27 at the time of his death and will still be sorely missed at the tournament in Brazil, with Ecuador retiring his number 11 jersey for qualifying matches as a tribute.

With just four games left to play in the South American group, Ecuador picked up only one point from their next two games in Colombia and Bolivia but rallied bravely back on home soil to claim a crucial 1–0 win over Uruguay, which manager Reinaldo Rueda dedicated to Benitez.

A 2–1 defeat in Chile then proved good enough to help them edge out Uruguay for the fourth and final automatic qualifying place in this pool on goal difference – reaching the finals for the third time in the last four.

For Rueda, the closing stages had been doubly tough to get

COACH

REINALDO RUEDA
Colombia-born coach Reinaldo Rueda built his reputation during a successful spell in charge of his home nation's junior teams, guiding them to third place in the 2003 FIFA World Youth Championship and fourth in the FIFA U–17 World Cup that year. He also helped Colombia's senior side salvage some pride from their 2006 FIFA World Cup qualifying campaign after stepping in following a poor run of results, before leading Honduras to South Africa 2010.

A passionate and deep-thinking manager, Rueda will instil a strong work ethic and hope playing as a unit can help overcome more talented opposition.

Left to right: Ecuador: (top row) Segundo Castillo, Frickson Erazo, Alexander Dominguez, Jorge Guagua, Christian Noboa, Felipe Caicedo; (bottom row) Jefferson Montero, Juan Carlos Paredes, Antonio Valencia, Enner Valencia, Walter Ayovi.

STAR MAN

ANTONIO VALENCIA
(Luis Antonio Valencia Mosquera)
BORN: 4 August 1985
CLUB: Manchester Utd (England)
A strong winger with a blend of pace and power, Antonio Valencia worked his way up the football ladder the hard way, proving himself with El Nacional in Ecuador and Wigan Athletic in England before joining Manchester United in the summer of 2009.

Described by former Old Trafford manager Sir Alex Ferguson as an "honest, hard-working player who can tackle, run and beat a man", Valencia is always looking to set up chances for team-mates in attacking positions with accurate crosses and although quiet for a captain, he leads by example on the pitch.

on the road was against Uruguay in Montevideo and only in Buenos Aires did they lose by more than one goal.

Captain Antonio Valencia fits the profile of a typically athletic Ecuador player, with the powerfully-built winger having picked up a number of team and individual honours during his time with Manchester United.

Felipe Caicedo was their leading scorer in qualifying with seven goals and he also has experience of playing in Europe's top leagues in England, Portugal, Spain and now Russia with Lokomotiv Moscow, while veterans such as Walter Ayovi, Segundo Castillo and Edison Mendez give them stability at the back.

Eight years ago in Germany, Ecuador fought their way through to the last 16, beating Poland and Costa Rica before losing narrowly to England, and few teams will relish the prospect of taking them on in the heat of battle in Brazil.

through, as the Colombian coach also lost his father just four days before the Benitez tragedy, but his spirit epitomised that of the whole squad in overcoming such adversity. "We'll greatly miss such a complete player and also what he meant to us off the pitch, in terms of his harmony, happiness and ability to mediate in disputes," said Rueda. "He's left a massive void to fill.

"Dealing with the grief has been difficult but you just have to keep going. We experience the bad moments in life with great intensity but we also overcome them in the same way."

Ecuador have also shown they can cope with testing conditions on the field, picking up 22 of their 25 qualifying points in the rarefied air of Estadio Olimpico Atahualpa in Quito, the highest capital city in the world. Seven home wins and a draw with Argentina at that venue earned them a trip to Brazil, where many players are expected to suffer from fatigue in a hot and demanding environment, but La Tricolor should adapt admirably.

"The Ecuadorians are physically strong and are very tough to beat here," said Manchester City striker Sergio Aguero after visiting Quito with Argentina. "We suffered quite a lot."

Only claiming three points away from home will give cause for concern that Ecuador do not travel well, but one of their three draws

ONES TO WATCH

FELIPE CAICEDO
(Felipe Salvador Caicedo Corozo)
BORN: 5 September 1988
CLUB: Lokomotiv Moscow (Russia)
A left-footed forward who can play down the middle or on the wing, Felipe Caicedo impressed with Basel in Switzerland before spells with Manchester City, Malaga, Levante and Lokomotiv Moscow. He is nicknamed Rocky for his love of the boxing films and has the same tenacity as the leading character in that series.

CHRISTIAN NOBOA
(Christian Fernando Noboa Tello)
BORN: 9 April 1985
CLUB: Dynamo Moscow (Russia)
A versatile midfielder who can take on several roles, Christian Noboa helped Rubin Kazan to claim a first Russian Premier League title before also impressing with Dynamo Moscow. Especially dangerous from dead-ball situations, he has a happy knack of scoring important goals from free-kicks or the penalty spot.

GROUP E

FRANCE

LES BLEUS

Didier Deschamps was captain of France when they won the FIFA World Cup for the first time in their history in 1998. Now, as coach, he is aiming to repeat that success as *Les Bleus* look to avoid the internal unrest that blighted their previous campaign.

COACH

DIDIER DESCHAMPS

Experienced boss Didier Deschamps will have all the know-how required to win a FIFA World Cup having featured so prominently as a player in his country's victorious 1998 campaign.

Having also led Monaco to a UEFA Champions League final as manager before claiming the French Ligue 1 title while at Marseille, it is clear the 45-year-old has all the credentials to be a success in Brazil.

There is little doubt Deschamps may need a little luck on the way but, if he can get the best out of players such as Franck Ribery and Karim Benzema, there is no reason why he cannot emulate Franz Beckenbauer in lifting the trophy both as a manager and a player.

To say France's performances at the FIFA World Cup finals have been hit and miss since winning their first title in 1998 is certainly an understatement.

Four years after a Zinedine Zidane-inspired team sent the Champs-Elysees into pandemonium, *Les Bleus* arrived in Japan and Korea with the expectation of the world on their shoulders, having since added the UEFA European Championship crown to their trophy cabinet.

Following a shock defeat to outsiders Senegal in the opening match, though, the much-fancied Blues failed to win a group game, without scoring a goal in the process, and returned home early with their tails between their legs.

France returned to the FIFA World Cup finals in 2006 and, with far less expectation upon them, Raymond Domenech's men went all the way to the final only to miss out on penalties following David Trezeguet's decisive miss.

Their most recent appearance in 2010 ended badly again after striker Nicolas Anelka was sent home for abusing then manager Domenech and their campaign duly fell apart, leaving them bottom of Group A without a win.

Qualification for Brazil could not have been more difficult for Deschamp's men after being drawn in the same group as current world champions Spain but, despite

Left to right: France: (top row) Patrice Evra, Raphael Varane, Mamadou Sakho, Hugo Lloris, Paul Pogba; (bottom row) Yohan Cabaye, Blaise Matuidi, Mathieu Debuchy, Mathieu Valbuena, Franck Ribery, Karim Benzema.

FRANCK RIBERY

BORN: 7 April 1983
CLUB: Bayern Munich (Germany)
Being considered as a contender for the prestigious FIFA Ballon d'Or award alongside Lionel Messi and Cristiano Ronaldo provides some idea of how highly regarded Franck Ribery is in world football.

Having won the UEFA Champions League in 2013 with club side Bayern Munich, the playmaker will now have his sights firmly set on adding the FIFA World Cup to his impressive list of career achievements.

After already appearing in one FIFA World Cup final – the 2006 penalty shootout defeat to Italy – Ribery is no stranger on the biggest stage of all, but the talismanic forward will know his team's success will rely heavily on his own performances.

FRANCE AT THE FIFA WORLD CUP™

1930	1st round
1934	1st round
1938	Quarter-finals
1954	1st round
1958	3rd place
1966	1st round
1978	1st round
1982	4th place
1986	3rd place
1998	CHAMPIONS
2002	1st round
2006	Runners-up
2010	1st round

that setback, France just missed out on automatic qualification after Pedro's solitary goal was the difference in the group's big clash at the Stade de France.

Faced with a two-legged play-off against underdogs Ukraine, who only just missed out on automatic qualification themselves behind England in Group H, the French could have been forgiven for thinking they had one foot in Brazil but, following a crushing 2-0 defeat in Kiev in which Laurent Koscielny was sent off, the nation's media turned on the team.

Missing out on the FIFA World Cup finals was suddenly a very realistic prospect but, when it mattered most, Franck Ribery and his team-mates turned on the style back in Paris. An unlikely double from defender Mamadou Sakho and Karim Benzema's solitary strike secured a 3-0 win and a trip to Brazil.

Despite the minor first-leg blip, Deschamps' confidence in his team and his hopes for what they can

produce in Brazil were highlighted in his post-match comments in Paris as he looked ahead to his nation's 14th appearance at the FIFA World Cup finals.

"It's the magic of football – four ways we were very bad but the players responded well," he said.

"It was important for French football to be in Brazil. When we've

got the ingredients we can do great things".

Having already won the 2013 FIFA U-20 World Cup in Turkey, it is clear to see that a very bright future lies ahead for France, with the likes of Paul Pogba, Marseille starlet Florian Thauvin and St Etienne's highly-rated centre-back Kurt Zouma all providing their nation with much cause for optimism in the years ahead.

That said, 2014 should come a little early for the majority of those players and it remains to be seen if their seniors have the strength in depth to go all the way in Brazil and claim the trophy for just a second time in their history.

ONES TO WATCH

PAUL POGBA

BORN: 15 March 1993
CLUB: Juventus (Italy)
Deemed surplus to requirements at Manchester United, Paul Pogba moved to Italian giants Juventus before turning heads all over Europe and beyond with his starring performances in midfield. Drawing comparisons to fellow Frenchman and FIFA World Cup winner Patrick Vieira, Pogba has all the qualities to make an impact in Brazil.

KARIM BENZEMA

BORN: 19 December 1987
CLUB: Real Madrid (Spain)
Despite struggling with goals of late at international level, 26-year-old Karim Benzema continues to impress for Real Madrid where he boasts an impressive scoring record of almost one goal every two games. If France are to reach the semi-finals or even beyond, the former Lyon striker will need to hit the ground running in Brazil.

HONDURAS

LOS CATRACHOS

A rejuvenated squad with a blend of promising young talent and previous FIFA World Cup experience helped Honduras qualify for the Brazilian showpiece and the challenge now is to reproduce those mature performances to get beyond the group stage for the first time.

COACH

LUIS FERNANDO SUAREZ

Honduras may never have progressed beyond the group stage at the FIFA World Cup finals but coach Luis Fernando Suarez has.

The 54-year-old was in charge of the Ecuador team that reached the finals in Germany in 2006, when wins against Poland and Costa Rica saw them reach the round of 16, where they were beaten by England.

The former Colombia international took charge of Honduras in 2011 and was also in charge of the team that reached the quarter-finals at the London 2012 Olympic Games.

In domestic football, he won the Colombian title with Atletico Nacional in 1999.

Honduras are back at the FIFA World Cup finals for a third time and their results in qualifying suggest they are ready to cause a few surprises.

They are yet to win on football's biggest stage and departed South Africa four years ago with only one point and no goals to their name, but much has changed since then.

Reinaldo Rueda's reign as coach ended after the 2010 tournament and he was succeeded by Luis Fernando Suarez, who has given opportunities to the next generation of players and has so far reaped the reward.

Suarez was also in charge of the U-23 team at the London 2012 Olympic Games and their progress to the quarter-finals provided him with more encouragement to give youth a chance. It was at the Olympics that Houston Dynamo striker Jerry Bengtson made the football world sit up and take notice of his talent, scoring twice against Morocco and then grabbing the only goal as Honduras dumped out the gold-medal favourites Spain with a famous victory.

His fine form in front of goal continued during qualifying, a campaign which began with Honduras topping their group on goal difference in the third round of the CONCACAF preliminaries.

That momentum continued into the CONCACAF Hexagonal, starting with an impressive 2–1 victory at home to the United States thanks to a late winner from Bengtson, which sparked wild celebrations in San Pedro Sula.

Solid home form was a theme throughout qualifying and they remained unbeaten in 10 matches,

Above: Honduras line up before the 2-2 draw with Jamaica in Kingston that secured qualification.

STAR MAN

WILSON PALACIOS
(Wilson Roberto Palacios Suazo)
BORN: 29 July 1984
CLUB: Stoke City (England)
Midfielder Wilson Palacios is the most recognisable of the Honduras squad, having impressed in English football since first moving to Birmingham City on loan in 2007.

Known for his physical strength, formidable work-rate and tough tackling, Palacios proved there is more to his game during the qualifying campaign and his creativity in the middle of the pitch was a key factor in his team reaching Brazil. The highlight was his goal in the 2–2 draw with Panama, when he surged into the penalty area, nutmegged a defender and delicately chipped the goalkeeper.

to be selected in the same FIFA World Cup finals squad.

Left-back Emilio Izaguirre is another vastly experienced player due to his time in Scotland, where he was named SPL Player of the Year following his debut season at Celtic in 2010–11. He is a vital part of a defence which is well marshalled by goalkeeper and captain Noel Valladares, who is the second most-capped player in Honduras' history.

He has been his country's first-choice goalkeeper for over a decade and has now appeared in four FIFA World Cup qualifying campaigns, having made his debut in 2000.

Valladares impressed at the last FIFA World Cup finals, conceding only three goals during the group stage and being named man of the match after keeping a clean sheet in the stalemate with Switzerland.

He may need to produce similar performances if his team are to reach the knockout stage for the first time but, as Mexico will testify, Honduras should not be underestimated.

but the best result of the campaign – and arguably in their history – came in Mexico City in September 2013. With his side deservedly trailing 1–0 at the break, Suarez threw on a second striker and the move paid off. Two goals in three minutes from Bengtson and Carlos Costly turned the match around and Honduras held on to condemn Mexico to only their second home defeat in 78 FIFA World Cup qualifying matches.

Four points from the next two games left Honduras on the brink of booking their ticket to Brazil and the third automatic qualification place was secured in the final match of the campaign when they earned the point they needed in a 2–2 draw with Jamaica in Kingston.

The squad now has an exciting mix of youth and experience and looks better equipped to shine at the FIFA World Cup finals than on previous occasions.

Several of the older players have already proved they can perform on a big stage. Roger Espinoza was part of the Wigan Athletic team that lifted the FA Cup in England last year with a stunning victory over Manchester City at Wembley, while Wilson Palacios enjoyed UEFA Champions League football at Tottenham Hotspur before moving on to Stoke City in 2011.

Palacios also made history in South Africa four years ago when he and siblings Jerry and Johnny became the first trio of brothers

ONES TO WATCH

JERRY BENGTSON
(Jerry Ricardo Bengtson Bodden)
BORN: 8 April 1987
CLUB: Houston Dynamo (USA)
Jerry Bengtson's goals were crucial in Honduras returning to the FIFA World Cup finals and the talented striker will be the focus of their attacks. He has impressed in Major League Soccer since moving there in July 2012 and scored three goals at the London 2012 Olympics.

EMILIO IZAGUIRRE
(Emilio Arturo Izaguirre Giron)
BORN: 10 May 1986
CLUB: Celtic (Scotland)
The left-back appeared at the 2010 FIFA World Cup finals and secured a move to Scottish giants Celtic, where he enjoyed a superb debut season and was named Scottish Premier League Player of the Year. He is a solid defender and a useful attacking threat down the wing.

ARGENTINA

FIFA WORLD CUP
Brasil

LA ALBICELESTES

With the world's best player as captain, the confidence of an impressive qualifying campaign behind them and playing in their own continent, there are several factors to suggest Argentina could get their hands on the FIFA World Cup for a third time in Brazil.

Argentina will embark on their 11th successive FIFA World Cup finals as one of the strong favourites to gatecrash the home nation's big party, while multiple FIFA Ballon D'Or winner Lionel Messi will bid to end the debate over who is the greatest footballer of all time.

Diego Maradona was the last Argentinian to hold aloft the FIFA World Cup Trophy in 1986. It was the defining moment in the career of one of the greatest ever players, but the South American country's football-mad population is ready to hail a new king.

Barcelona superstar Messi could arguably supplant both Maradona and Pele at the top of the all-time list if he can inspire a golden generation and lay his hands on the trophy in Rio de Janeiro.

But unlike Maradona's triumph in Mexico City 28 years ago, Argentina's 2014 challenge will not be a one-man show.

Messi's genius will be harnessed alongside the offensive triumvirate of Manchester City striker Sergio Aguero, winger Angel Di Maria of Real Madrid and Napoli centre-forward Gonzalo Higuain.

Should any part of that dazzling quartet misfire, coach Alejandro Sabella can call on Juventus forward Carlos Tevez, Paris Saint-Germain winger Ezequiel Lavezzi or his club team-mate and attacking midfielder Javier Pastore. Any combination has the potential to dismantle the world's best-organised defences.

La Albicelestes cruised through their South American qualifiers to book their place at the 2014 FIFA World Cup with two games to spare and have an abundance of genuine match-winners in their squad. Sabella has promised that, unlike 1986, it will be more of a

COACH

ALEJANDRO SABELLA
Alejandro Sabella embarks on his first FIFA World Cup finals as national team manager and although not the popular choice to succeed Sergio Batista in August 2011, he has already won over many of his critics.

Sabella was on Argentina's coaching staff at the 1998 FIFA World Cup, has coached Uruguay and rose to prominence as a manager in his own right in guiding Estudiantes to Copa Libertadores glory in 2009.

A meticulous planner and charismatic man-manager, Sabella has gelled a golden generation of great talents into a well-organised team.

Left to right: Argentina: (top row) Jose Basanta, Sergio Romero, Fabricio Coloccini, Hugo Campagnaro, Fernando Gago; (bottom row) Lionel Messi, Angel Di Maria, Sergio Aguero, Pablo Zabaleta, Lucas Biglia, Rodrigo Palacio.

STAR MAN

LIONEL MESSI

BORN: 24 June 1987
CLUB: Barcelona (Spain)

Lionel Messi is undoubtedly the greatest player of his generation and has taken the game to new heights during a glittering decade for club side Barcelona.

His ability to run with the ball and change direction while at top speed make him a nightmare for defenders and he continues to break countless records with his stunning goalscoring feats.

Many commentators hail him as the greatest player of all time despite his failure, so far, to win the FIFA World Cup.

team effort, albeit geared to get the best out of Messi.

At the 2006 FIFA World Cup in Germany, a teenage Messi played a cameo role under then coach Jose Pekerman, who left him on the bench when Argentina were knocked out by the host nation in a quarter-final penalty shootout.

Four years later in South Africa, national treasure Maradona had returned as coach, but his fixation on Messi and gung-ho approach were exposed in the quarter-finals, again by Germany, whose well-balanced side triumphed 4–0.

This time around, the savvy Sabella, who succeeded Sergio Batista as coach in August 2011 following Argentina's disappointing quarter-final exit in the Copa America, still has Messi as the focal point – he installed him as captain – but with a fundamental difference; Messi is one part of the team.

Sabella has put the emphasis on the collective rather than any individual and, as a consequence, cohesion and team spirit blossomed during the impressive qualifying campaign.

For too long Argentina have been found wanting both tactically and defensively. No team, reasoned

Sabella, can expect to triumph in Brazil without a solid foundation.

"Overhauling the defence has taken a bit more time, that's true," he said. "We need to stay grounded about it, but when you've got strikers of the quality of Messi, Higuain and Aguero, I don't think people should be offended by anyone saying the back line is proving to be a bit more of a headache."

Big central defenders Ezequiel Garay and Federico Fernandez have provided the perfect tonic, emerging through qualifying as

Sabella's twin towers. Together with full-backs Pablo Zabaleta and Marcos Rojo, they offer goalkeeper Sergio Romero much-improved protection behind an industrious midfield hub that includes the likes of Fernando Gago, Javier Mascherano and Ever Banega.

Messi has occasionally struggled to replicate his astronomical Barcelona form when representing Argentina, but under Sabella he no longer has to chase his tail.

He has well-drilled, world-class performers all around him and the stage is set for the little sorcerer to finally settle that argument.

ONES TO WATCH

EZEQUIEL GARAY

BORN: 10 October 1986
CLUB: Benfica (Portugal)

Much has been made of Argentina's attack, but Ezequiel Garay has played a key role in their transformation into genuine FIFA World Cup contenders. The former Real Madrid defender, close to joining Manchester United in the summer of 2013, is a towering presence and has matured into a technically gifted centre-back.

EZEQUIEL LAVEZZI

BORN: 3 May 1985
CLUB: Paris Saint-Germain (France)

Winger or striker Ezequiel Lavezzi has all the attributes required to terrorise defenders, with plenty of pace, strength, quick feet and an excellent cross. Dubbed the 'new Maradona' by the Italian media shortly after joining former club Napoli in 2007, Paris Saint-Germain paid a reported €30m for him in June 2012.

BOSNIA-HERZEGOVINA

 **FIFA WORLD CUP** Brasil

THE DRAGONS

Celebrations in Sarajevo lasted for days when Bosnia-Herzegovina qualified for the 2014 FIFA World Cup finals with victory over Lithuania in October. Safet Susic had steered the nation to its first major tournament since independence from Yugoslavia, and now aims to make more history.

COACH

SAFET SUSIC

Safet Susic has already achieved legendary status in his homeland by guiding Bosnia-Herzegovina to their first major tournament but the former Paris Saint-Germain midfielder retains even loftier ambitions.

He replaced Miroslav Blazevic in 2009 and overcame a poor start to secure a UEFA EURO 2012 qualifying play-off against Portugal, which saw Bosnia-Herzegovina beaten 6–2 over two legs. It was that disappointment that inspired Susic and his beloved nation to greater things.

His flamboyant system helped Bosnia-Herzegovina outscore main rivals Greece in Group G and, despite the wobble of a home defeat to Slovakia, he successfully steered the Dragons over the line and towards Brazil with confident closing victories over Liechtenstein and Lithuania.

When the full-time whistle blew on Bosnia-Herzegovina's 1–0 victory over Lithuania in Kaunas, a young nation's mission to reach a major tournament was over after nearly 20 years of struggle. The former Yugoslav state had outperformed European powerhouses Greece and recent FIFA World Cup competitors Slovakia to reach the finals in Brazil, with no small amount of style.

Thirty goals were scored and only six conceded as a dynamic and ruthless side stunned their rivals, scoring at least three goals in six of their 10 qualifying matches and reaching 13th place in the FIFA/Coca-Cola World Ranking, their highest ever position.

Between August 2012 and August 2013, coach Safet Susic – a star of the 1980s Yugoslavia team – oversaw a nine-match unbeaten run on the international stage.

No campaign is without its obstacles though, and Bosnia-Herzegovina needed a late rally to pip Greece to top spot and book their tickets to Brazil, consigning the 2004 European champions to the play-offs.

Tirana was the setting for Bosnia-Herzegovina's first appointment as a FIFA-recognised nation but they left Albania on the back of a 2–0 defeat in November 1995. Full FIFA membership followed a year later and the former Yugoslav nation steadily began to grow in confidence and in stature.

It was not until the qualifying campaign for UEFA EURO 2004 that Bosnia-Herzegovina really

Left to right: Bosnia-Herzegovina: (top row) Sejad Salihovic, Elvir Rahimic, Vedad Ibisevic, Ervin Zukanovic, Edin Dzeko, Asmir Begovic; (bottom row) Haris Medunjanin, Miralem Pjanic, Mensur Mujdza, Senad Lulic, Emir Spahic.

STAR MAN

EDIN DZEKO

BORN: 17 March 1986
CLUB: Manchester City (England)

Edin Dzeko may have struggled for regular first-team football at Manchester City but there is no denying the imposing frontman is the star for Bosnia-Herzegovina.

Ever since he captured the nation's imagination with a sublime volley on his senior debut against Turkey, the man dubbed 'the Bosnian Diamond' has rattled in goals for his country on a regular basis. He scored nine during qualifying for the 2010 FIFA World Cup and went one better during the historic 2014 qualifying campaign, finishing second only to the Netherlands' Robin van Persie in the European scoring charts.

His hat-trick against Liechtenstein saw him become Bosnia-Herzegovina's all-time leading scorer as he passed Elvir Bolic's total of 22 goals.

BOSNIA-HERZEGOVINA AT THE FIFA WORLD CUP™

FIFA World Cup 2014 will be Bosnia-Herzegovina's first finals appearance since their independence from Yugoslavia.

their incisive attacking play. "We'll be one of the smallest nations," he said. "We'll go and enjoy the experience and try to cause a couple of upsets.

"We don't want to just make up the numbers. We want to compete and see if we can achieve something and give even more happiness to our people and our nation."

However far Bosnia-Herzegovina manage to go in Brazil, any positive experience in a summer tournament will lift the spirits of a Balkan nation that is still struggling to recover from the regional conflicts of the 1990s.

Begovic added: "It's the best thing that's ever happened to the nation. It's nice to have something good happen to Bosnia.

"After all the tough times in the past – and some things that are still going on now – it's really nice to give them that bit of joy and something to cherish and cheer."

began to make their presence felt on the continent, but a series of near-misses meant they would have to wait until October 2009 to contest a play-off for the first time.

Portugal denied the Dragons a place at the 2010 FIFA World Cup finals and proved far too strong for Susic's side in another play-off ahead of UEFA EURO 2012, triumphing 6–2 over two legs to inspire a dramatic rethink in the Bosnia-Herzegovina camp.

The subsequent emergence of playmaker Miralem Pjanic and an increased goal return from Edin Dzeko, who hit the back of the net 10 times in qualifying for Brazil, were key to Bosnia-Herzegovina finishing at the top of Group G on goal difference.

A tough defence marshalled by long-serving captain Emir Spahic and safeguarded by goalkeeper Asmir Begovic was also vital and will need to remain resilient against

the world's leading strikers in South America.

While Begovic knows it will be a tall order to keep clean sheets in Brazil, he insists his team-mates are more interested in upsetting the established world order with

ONES TO WATCH

MIRALEM PJANIC

BORN: 2 April 1990
CLUB: Roma (Italy)

Mercurial midfielder Miralem Pjanic announced himself as one of Europe's most promising talents during three seasons with Lyon but it has been with Italian giants Roma that he has truly blossomed. As deadly in and around the box as he is from set-pieces, Pjanic provides creative spark and cutting edge in equal measure.

ASMIR BEGOVIC

BORN: 20 June 1987
CLUB: Stoke City (England)

As the second of two Bosnians playing in the English Premier League – along with Edin Dzeko – Asmir Begovic enjoys a growing reputation as one of the most resilient goalkeepers in Europe. The Stoke stopper kept four clean sheets during the qualifying campaign and adds further steel and leadership to an already fearsome backline.

IRAN

FIFA WORLD CUP Brasil

TEAM MELLI

Iran head to the FIFA World Cup finals for the fourth time in their history and with experienced Portuguese coach Carlos Queiroz in charge, Team Melli are looking to build on an impressive qualifying campaign and establish themselves as one of the best teams in Asian football.

COACH

CARLOS QUEIROZ

Iran's squad may lack experience on the biggest stage but the same cannot be said of coach Carlos Queiroz. Having managed home nation Portugal twice, including at the 2010 FIFA World Cup in South Africa, and helping South Africa qualify for the 2002 finals, Queiroz is no stranger to the pressure that awaits his team in Brazil. At club level, Queiroz has coached some of the greatest players in the world – including Zinedine Zidane, Luis Figo and Ronaldo – during spells as head coach of Real Madrid and assistant to Sir Alex Ferguson at Manchester United. He took over as Iran coach in April 2011, signing a two-and-a-half-year contract to the end of the 2014 FIFA World Cup.

There were wild celebrations on the streets of Tehran when Iran qualified for the 2014 FIFA World Cup and those scenes could be repeated if they can reach the knockout stage for the first time.

This is the fourth time Iran have qualified for the FIFA World Cup finals and the challenge for coach Carlos Queiroz and Team Melli is now to go one step further than their predecessors.

The way in which they booked their ticket to Brazil by topping Group A in the Asian qualifiers certainly bodes well, after winning five of their eight matches and conceding only two goals. A well-organised defence provided a solid platform and the introduction of Reza Ghoochannejhad was an inspired move by Queiroz as the Standard Liege striker's lethal form in front of goal proved decisive.

Two single-goal victories against the much-fancied Korea Republic highlighted Iran's ability. They were roared on by almost 100,000 patriotic fans for the home success in Tehran, before Ghoochannejhad's winner sealed a famous win in the final group game in Ulsan and ensured they qualified as group winners.

Above: Iran's players celebrate the second win over Korea Republic in Ulsan to seal qualification.

STAR MAN

REZA GHOOCHANNEJHAD

(Reza Ghoochannejhad Nournia)
BORN: 20 September 1987
CLUB: Standard Liege (Belgium)
Iran's qualification for Brazil owes much to the goals of Reza Ghoochannejhad, or Gucci as he is better known by the fans.

Having moved to the Netherlands as a child after being born in Iran, the striker was plying his trade in in Belgium when he was spotted by Carlos Queiroz during a scouting mission being carried out by the national coach.

Ghoochannejhad made his debut in a 1–0 victory against Korea Republic in October 2012 but shot to prominence later in the qualifying campaign with three vital goals in as many games, including the winners against Qatar and Korea Republic to ensure qualification.

Supporters back home took to the streets for the second time in four days, with the win coming just four days after the presidential election victory of Hassan Rowhani and adding to the feel-good factor in the country. The new president even joined in the celebrations, posting a message on Twitter which read: "Congratulations to my dear people on the occasion of our qualification for the 2014 FIFA World Cup Brazil. So proud of our national team!" Around 40,000 fans then welcomed the team at the airport on their arrival back in Tehran as a feeling of national pride swept the country.

Iran first appeared at the FIFA World Cup finals in 1978 when they ended their campaign with a creditable draw against Scotland following defeats by the Netherlands and Peru. It was 20 years before they appeared at the finals again but it proved worth the wait as Iran secured an historic 2–1 win against the United States.

Two defeats and a draw with Angola followed at the 2006 FIFA World Cup in Germany and now, eight years later, they hope to take their football to a new level.

The appointment of former Real Madrid and Portugal head coach Queiroz was a shrewd move and Iran's success saw him enter the history books as the first Portuguese coach to have secured consecutive FIFA World Cup qualifications after taking his home country to the 2010 FIFA World Cup South Africa.

Discipline and team spirit were important factors in Iran's approach and will be sure to continue in Brazil, with Queiroz aiming to now establish Iran as one of the top three sides in Asian football, alongside Japan and Korea Republic.

Using the excitement of the FIFA World Cup to create a footballing legacy in the country is also a stated aim of Queiroz, who is hoping an improvement in the standard of competition, coaching and facilities in Iran will all follow when the samba drums of Brazil become a fading memory.

ONES TO WATCH

JAVAD NEKONAM
BORN: 7 September 1980
CLUB: Esteghlal (Iran)
The Iran captain is a survivor from the team which competed at the 2006 FIFA World Cup in Germany and, with more than 130 caps to his name, brings a wealth of experience to the squad. The central midfielder spent much of his career with Osasuna in Spain before returning to his native country in 2012.

ASHKAN DEJAGAH
(Seyed Ashkan Dejagah)
BORN: 5 July 1986
CLUB: Fulham (England)
A talented wide midfielder with flair and pace, Ashkan Dejagah played for Germany at every age level from under 17s to under 21s but became eligible to play for Iran and scored twice on his debut against Qatar in 2012. After three years at Hertha Berlin, he moved to Wolfsburg before joining Fulham in 2012.

NIGERIA

THE SUPER EAGLES

The Super Eagles of Nigeria travel to South America with high hopes as they look to build on their third triumph in the CAF Africa Cup of Nations in early 2013 by going further than ever before in what will be their fifth appearance at the FIFA World Cup finals.

COACH

STEPHEN KESHI

After becoming the first Nigerian to lead the Super Eagles to victory at the CAF Africa Cup of Nations in 2013, Stephen Keshi will be looking to make further history when he heads to his first FIFA World Cup finals as a manager.

Keshi shot to prominence when he steered Togo to qualification for the 2006 FIFA World Cup finals but, following a disappointing CAF African Cup of Nations campaign, Keshi was denied the opportunity to manage at the tournament when he was replaced by Otto Pfister in February 2006. Keshi captained Nigeria at the 1994 competition and will be hoping his FIFA World Cup experience can help the current crop of players reach new heights in Brazil.

After ending their 19-year wait to lift the CAF Africa Cup of Nations trophy in 2013, Nigeria are brimming with confidence and are ready to show the world what they are capable of on the biggest stage of all.

The Super Eagles have struggled at recent FIFA World Cup tournaments but with former captain Stephen Keshi at the helm, the African champions are an entirely different proposition this time around.

Since he was appointed in 2011, Keshi has earned widespread praise for his policy of picking home-based talent rather than naming an entire squad of players who ply their trade in Europe's top leagues. Many fans raised an eyebrow when Enugu Rangers midfielder Sunday Mba was named in Keshi's CAF Africa Cup of Nations squad ahead of better-known players such as Dynamo Kyiv's Lukman Haruna, but Mba then went on to score the only goal in the final as Nigeria beat Burkina Faso.

Keshi's strategy has reinvigorated the national team and created a real buzz among football fans in Nigeria, so much so that key figures in the country truly believe their side has what it takes to win the most sought-after trophy in world football.

After watching Keshi's side cruise to a 4–1 aggregate victory over Ethiopia in their qualification play-off clash, Nigeria president

Left to right: Nigeria: (top row) John Obi Mikel, Kenneth Omeruo, Brown Ideye, Emmanuel Emenike, Godfrey Oboabona, Efe Ambrose; (bottom row) Victor Moses, Elderson Echieille, Vincent Enyeama, Ogenyi Onazi, Ahmed Musa.

STAR MAN

JOHN OBI MIKEL
(John Michael Nchekwube Obinna)

BORN: 22 April 1987
CLUB: Chelsea (England)

John Obi Mikel may not be a prolific goalscorer, but what the Chelsea man does bring to the team makes him one of Nigeria's most prized assets. Mikel is a tough-tackling midfield general who never shies away from putting in a challenge. Not only does he provide vital cover for the back four, Mikel has a remarkable ability to turn defence into attack.

Mikel has never been to the FIFA World Cup finals as he missed the last tournament through injury, but he is not short of international experience. He has played more than 50 games for his country since making his debut in 2005 and was a key player for the Super Eagles during their CAF Africa Cup of Nations-winning campaign in 2013.

NIGERIA AT THE FIFA WORLD CUP™

1994	Round of 16
1998	Round of 16
2002	1st round
2010	1st round

Goodluck Jonathan put forward his view that the Super Eagles are even capable of winning the FIFA World Cup.

He told FIFA.com: "With the enormous pool of footballing talent available to the country, the Super Eagles can, with more hard work, dedication, resilience and further honing of their skills and tactics, fulfil the national dream of being the first African nation to win the World Cup."

It could be argued that the president's talk of winning the competition does nothing but put unnecessary pressure on the players, but many of them welcome such comments. In fact, some of the squad's most senior players agree with him.

Goalkeeper and captain Vincent Enyeama also thinks his side can go all the way in Brazil.

"(Will we) make an impression at the World Cup? No, we can actually win it," he insisted. "I wouldn't be surprised if Nigeria win the World Cup one day – maybe with me. It's just a matter of time and moment. Everything is possible. Impossible is nothing."

Nigeria certainly have a good chance of making the quarter-finals for the first time. They have a young and hungry squad but one thing many of the players lack is FIFA World Cup experience. One man in their ranks who is not short of this is Keshi.

In 1994, Nigeria travelled to the United States to take part in their first FIFA World Cup finals. As with today's national team, many of the players were young and inexperienced, but the Super Eagles were lucky enough to have an older and wiser player to lead the likes of Daniel Amokachi, Victor Ikpeba and Sunday Oliseh, all of whom were 21 or younger. That man was Stephen Keshi.

Nigeria shocked the world of football in 1994, finishing top of their group ahead of Argentina, Bulgaria and Greece. They may have gone out of the competition in the second round, losing to eventual runners-up Italy in extra time, but the Super Eagles gave an excellent account of themselves.

Now Keshi will be hoping to go even further when he takes Nigeria's current crop of young players to Brazil.

ONES TO WATCH

VICTOR MOSES
BORN: 12 December 1990
CLUB: Chelsea (England)

Chelsea's Victor Moses is a powerful forward with incredible pace and a deadly eye for goal. The Lagos-born marksman, who won the 2013 Nigerian Player of the Year award, will be looking to make a big impact when he heads to his first ever FIFA World Cup finals.

EFE AMBROSE
(Efetobore Ambrose Emuobo)
BORN: 18 October 1988
CLUB: Celtic (Scotland)

Not only is Celtic centre-back Efe Ambrose good in the air but he is very comfortable with the ball at his feet. The 25-year-old can play anywhere across the back four but he is also capable in front of goal and poses a real threat at the other end.

GERMANY

DIE MANNSCHAFT

**FIFA WORLD CUP
Brasil**

Germany head to Brazil aiming to end a trio of near misses at FIFA World Cup finals. With a shrewd boss overseeing a star-studded squad, the Germans appear to have all the requirements to end 24 years of hurt, having last won the competition in 1990.

COACH

JOACHIM LOW

Ever since Jurgen Klinsmann succeeded Rudi Voeller in 2004 and quickly installed former midfielder Joachim Low as his assistant coach, the latter has had a huge say in changing the philosophy of the three-time FIFA World Cup winners.

The pair transformed the Germans into a more attacking outfit, showing glimpses of their potential in front of their own fans in 2006 and, after Klinsmann opted not to renew his contract, Low was given a promotion.

He blooded younger players and they have repaid his faith with an array of stunning performances since, most notably in routs of England and Argentina in South Africa four years ago.

Despite being regarded as one of the world's most feared footballing nations, Germany's fourth FIFA World Cup success has proved somewhat elusive.

They have gone agonisingly close over the last 12 years, finishing runners-up to Brazil in Korea/Japan in 2002 before suffering semi-final exits at the hands of Italy in their homeland in 2006 and Spain in South Africa four years later.

However, under the leadership of Joachim Low, Die Mannschaft are one of the favourites to triumph in South America after again showing their class during an unbeaten qualifying campaign.

Their remarkable record of having lost only twice in FIFA World Cup qualifying campaigns – to Portugal in 1985 and England six years later – was extended following nine wins and a draw in Group C this time.

One of the main reasons for Germany's impressive showings over recent years has been the influence of Low. The former Stuttgart boss introduced the likes of goalkeeper Manuel Neuer, midfielder Sami Khedira and playmaker Mesut Ozil, who have all become outstanding performers for their clubs and country since.

Together with the experience of striker Miroslav Klose, midfielder Bastian Schweinsteiger and versatile skipper Philipp Lahm, and emerging players such as forwards Mario Goetze and Marco Reus, Germany have the ability to win the 2014 FIFA World Cup.

It is no coincidence that a number of Low's squad have excelled for their club sides over

Above: Germany line up before their qualifying game against the Republic of Ireland.

STAR MAN

BASTIAN SCHWEINSTEIGER

BORN: 1 August 1984
CLUB: Bayern Munich (Germany)

Bastian Schweinsteiger has been around for a number of years and continues to lead by example on the field for both club and country.

After starting his career as a winger, he has adapted to a central role and makes the game look easy with his range of passing, excellent vision, superb positioning, precise ball control and ability to tackle.

When Germany need inspiration, Schweinsteiger steps up and takes charge, with his driving runs a constant threat.

GERMANY AT THE FIFA WORLD CUP™

1934	3rd place
1938	1st round
1954	CHAMPIONS
1958	4th place
1962	Quarter-finals
1966	Runners-up
1970	3rd place
1974	CHAMPIONS
1978	2nd round
1982	Runners-up
1986	Runners-up
1990	CHAMPIONS
1994	Quarter-finals
1998	Quarter-finals
2002	Runners-up
2006	3rd place
2010	3rd place

the last few years, in both domestic and European competitions, with Bundesliga rivals Bayern Munich and Borussia Dortmund facing each other in the 2013 UEFA Champions League final.

Veteran Klose has been an integral part of their success, netting 14 times in FIFA World Cup finals, and heads to South America looking to surpass Brazil striker Ronaldo's tally of 15 in what will be his last international tournament.

Klose is heading towards the latter stages of his career but adds valuable experience. Thomas Mueller, who won the adidas Golden Boot and Best Young Player awards four years ago, adds to the attacking options along with Max Kruse, Mario Gomez, Stefan Kiessling and Lukas Podolski.

Asked if his squad has the potential to be the best German side ever, Low – whose reward for leading his country to Brazil was a two-year contract extension – said: "I look at previous campaigns, especially during Euro 2012. The team is more solid, more stable and more compact in defence. I used this campaign to make my team more stable. It hinges around the opponent you play, they will

have a major role in making games attractive or nice to watch for the spectators. Of course we do have some things to tackle. Defensively, there is room for improvement. But the matches against Austria and Ireland really came close to perfection."

Despite Germany scoring the most goals in European qualifying, their defence has suffered as a result of their attacking approach and needs to improve if they are to go all the way. Their only draw in qualifying came when they remarkably threw away a four-goal lead in the final 30 minutes

to be held 4–4 by Sweden, who also breached the German defence three times in the return, while also leaking goals in friendlies against South American sides. Low said: "Four-four after being 4–0 up, you will not be the media darling for that weekend. We had to take the flak for conceding four in a row."

Since August 2012, the Germans have conceded twice against Ecuador, three times versus Paraguay and Argentina and shipped four goals in a defeat to the United States, which means improvements are still needed if they are to be world champions for the first time since 1990.

ONES TO WATCH

MESUT OZIL

BORN: 15 October 1988
CLUB: Arsenal (England)

In Mesut Ozil, Germany have one of the best playmakers in the world. Roaming in the space between midfield and attack, the Arsenal player's vision to pick a pass leaves defences exposed and hands strikers such as Miroslav Klose and Thomas Mueller chances on a plate.

PHILIPP LAHM

BORN: 11 November 1983
CLUB: Bayern Munich (Germany)

Influential in a number of positions, Philipp Lahm's consistency is second to none. Whether at full-back or in midfield, where he has been operating under Pep Guardiola at Bayern Munich, Lahm's energy and ability to keep possession make him a key man.

PORTUGAL

SELECAO DAS QUINAS

Portugal endured a rocky road to Brazil but will embark on their sixth FIFA World Cup finals with optimism mainly because of the man ultimately responsible for getting them there – Real Madrid superstar Cristiano Ronaldo.

COACH

PAULO BENTO

Paulo Bento succeeded Carlos Queiroz as national-team coach in 2010 following four highly successful years in charge of Sporting Lisbon and he guided Portugal to the semi-finals of UEFA EURO 2012 in his first major tournament.

Renowned as a tough-tackling midfielder in his playing days, Bento was banned from international football for five months for his part in the man-handling of the referee during the UEFA EURO 2000 semi-final defeat to France. He won 35 caps, with his last coming at the 2002 FIFA World Cup.

He developed a reputation as a cautious coach with Sporting but his stock is rising after transforming the national side's fortunes.

Cristiano Ronaldo is a football phenomenon and while the hopes of a nation rest on his shoulders, millions of admirers the world over were grateful his stunning hat-trick in Portugal's play-off victory over Sweden secured him his rightful place on the biggest stage.

Portugal lost only once in their qualifying group but finishing second behind Russia condemned them to the play-offs.

Ronaldo had for years been criticised for failing to replicate his stellar performances at Real Madrid for his country when it really mattered, but the former Manchester United ace delivered.

His crucial late winner in the first leg in Lisbon gave Portugal a 1–0 lead to defend in Solna and he struck the opening goal in the return leg to put his side in control. Sweden's superstar Zlatan Ibrahimovic then scored twice in four minutes to tip the tie back in the balance but no matter, Ronaldo duly scored two more.

The 29-year-old's trademark hat-trick – he was the only player to score two of them in the FIFA World Cup qualifying campaign – saw him outshine Ibrahimovic and equal Portugal's all-time leading goalscorer Pauleto on 47.

It also prompted many of the world's leading players to declare Ronaldo had finally sealed his place as the best footballer on the planet. Eclipsed by four-time FIFA Ballon d'Or winner Lionel Messi for so long, Ronaldo at last received the acclaim his talents deserved. Real Madrid coach Carlo

Left to right: Portugal: (top row) Nani, Hugo Almeida, Bruno Alves, Cristiano Ronaldo, Pepe, Rui Patricio; (bottom row) Joao Moutinho, Fabio Coentrao, Joao Pereira, Raul Meireles, Miguel Veloso.

STAR MAN

CRISTIANO RONALDO

(Cristiano Ronaldo dos Santos Aveiro)

BORN: 5 February 1985
CLUB: Real Madrid (Spain)

Cristiano Ronaldo silenced the critics who claim he rarely produces his best on the international stage in spectacular fashion in the qualifying play-off win over Sweden by scoring all four of Portugal's goals over two legs.

Ronaldo and Lionel Messi stand head and shoulders above their contemporaries in world football after taking the art of goalscoring to new levels and both will hope to prove they are the greatest player of their generation with their performances in Brazil. He became the world's most expensive player when he joined Real Madrid from Manchester United in 2009.

is capable of shackling the world's best strikers along with Real Madrid team-mate Fabio Coentrao.

Portugal qualified for their first FIFA World Cup finals in 1966 when legendary striker Eusebio led them to the semi-finals, where they lost to eventual winners England, and they have an impressive record in more recent competitions.

Their 'golden generation' of Luis Figo, Nuno Gomes, Rui Costa, Fernando Couto and Paulo Sousa reached the semi-finals of UEFA EURO 2000, were runners-up four years later and were knocked out by France in the last four at the FIFA World Cup finals in 2006.

Spain ended Portugal's 19-game unbeaten run under former coach Carlos Queiroz in the last-16 stage of the 2010 FIFA World Cup finals. Ronaldo, stifled by the weight of expectation, had failed to fire and Queiroz was sacked soon after, to be replaced by Bento. If he can get the best out of his star player, Portugal could go far.

Ancelotti summed it up when he said: "He scores so regularly and with such incredible ease. It's hard to find new words to describe him. Cristiano's talent puts him in a different category altogether."

Ronaldo may be by some distance Portugal's star attraction in Brazil, but familiar names are not in short supply and after leading the nation to the semi-finals of UEFA EURO 2012, coach Paulo Bento has plenty of other reasons to be confident of more success.

Monaco's central midfielder Joao Moutinho was arguably Portugal's outstanding player at UEFA EURO 2012, where Bento's side lost to eventual winners Spain in a semi-final penalty shootout. Moutinho's ball retention and distribution are among the best and he was linked with a move to Chelsea in 2013 before heading from Porto to the French Riviera.

Fellow midfielder Raul Meireles – a UEFA Champions League winner with Chelsea – has more than 70 caps for Portugal and his energy is integral to Bento's plans.

Manchester United winger Nani has also proved to be a world-class performer on his day and is an ideal foil for Ronaldo, who often has licence to roam off the opposite flank.

Portugal leaked too many goals in qualifying – they conceded one against minnows Luxembourg and three in Israel – and it cost them an automatic place in Brazil, but Pepe

ONES TO WATCH

WILLIAM CARVALHO

(William Silva de Carvalho)

BORN: 7 April 1992
CLUB: Sporting Lisbon (Portugal)

The young midfielder only made his debut in the second leg of the play-off against Sweden but has been ear-marked to form the bedrock of future Portugal teams, demonstrating maturity and composure beyond his years. It appears only a matter of time before he makes the defensive midfield role his own.

LUIS NETO

(Luis Carlos Novo Neto)

BORN: 26 May 1988
CLUB: Zenit St Petersburg (Russia)

Luis Neto is another blossoming talent ready to make the step up to Paulo Bento's starting line-up. The central defender caught the eye in Italy's Serie A before relegation forced Siena to sell him at the end of the 2012–13 season to Zenit St Petersburg, where he has maintained his rise to stardom.

GHANA

FIFA WORLD CUP
Brasil

BLACK STARS

Success at the top level often comes down to fine margins and no team knows that more than Ghana. Only an infamous handball and subsequent penalty miss denied them a semi-final place four years ago but they will hope to enjoy better luck in a third successive FIFA World Cup finals.

COACH

KWESI APPIAH

Kwesi Appiah made history by becoming the first black African coach to qualify for the FIFA World Cup finals following the 7-3 aggregate success against Egypt in the play-offs.

He was an assistant coach of the national team from 2008 and took overall charge in 2012 after the failure to reach the CAF Africa Nations Cup final prompted the dismissal of Goran Stevanovic.

Appiah captained Ghana during his playing days as a left-back and although he lacks managerial experience at the highest level, he guided Ghana U-23s to success at the All Africa Games in 2011.

Ghana have found themselves flying the flag for African football at the previous two FIFA World Cup finals and their impressive form in qualifying suggests that could be the case once again.

They were the only team from the continent to get beyond the group stage in both 2006 and 2010, and the manner of their exit in South Africa four years ago means they have unfinished business on the world stage.

The Black Stars looked set to be Africa's first ever FIFA World Cup semi-finalists when a Luis Suarez handball on the line presented them with a last-minute extra-time penalty against Uruguay. Asamoah

Gyan agonisingly missed the spot-kick though – his shot crashing against the crossbar – and Uruguay won the subsequent shootout to eliminate Ghana in the cruellest of circumstances.

Despite that disappointment, there was much for Ghana to be proud of.

Only two African countries – Cameroon in 1990 and Senegal in 2002 – had previously reached the last eight and Ghana's current squad remains full of established names who could prove to be more than a match for the top sides this time around.

Gyan became the first player to miss two penalties in the FIFA

Left to right: Ghana: (top row) Kwadwo Asamoah, Michael Essien, Rashid Sumaila, Fatawu Dauda, Andre Ayew, Jerry Akaminko; (bottom row) Asamoah Gyan, Harrison Afful, Daniel Opare, Majeed Waris, Sulley Muntari.

STAR MAN

MICHAEL ESSIEN
BORN: 3 December 1982
CLUB: Chelsea (England)

Tough-tackling midfielder Michael Essien would be a major asset to any club and he certainly has been throughout his nine-year career with Chelsea, who made him the most expensive African footballer at the time when they signed him in 2005.

He won two English Premier League titles with the Blues but spent the 2012–13 season on loan at Spanish giants Real Madrid under Jose Mourinho before the Portuguese manager's move back to Stamford Bridge.

Essien made his Ghana debut in 2002 and featured at the 2006 FIFA World Cup finals but was absent in 2010 due to a knee injury.

GHANA AT THE FIFA WORLD CUP™

2006...................Round of 16
2010................Quarter-finals

World Cup but he is now a man on a mission and high on confidence heading into Ghana's third appearance at the finals.

"My football career is going well right now," he told FIFA.com. "At international level I couldn't be happier with how things are going for Ghana right now too. I'm enjoying my life and I'm enjoying the game."

Gyan's goals will again be crucial – he was the joint-top scorer in the African preliminaries with six – but much of their success has been thanks to their midfield where they have talent and experience in abundance.

Michael Essien has proved to be one of the best midfielders in the world during his time at Chelsea and Real Madrid, while other big names include the likes of AC Milan's Sulley Muntari, Marseille's Andre Ayew and Kevin-Prince Boateng of Schalke 04.

Ghana faced a tough group in the second round of CAF qualifying alongside Zambia, Lesotho and Sudan, but made a dream start with a 7-0 win against Lesotho. A 1–0 loss to Zambia then proved to be only a minor setback as they bounced back with four straight wins to ease into the third round and their 25 goals made them the most prolific of the African teams.

On paper they looked to have been given a tough draw after being paired with seven-times African champions Egypt but their prolific form in front of goal continued as they effectively ended the contest on home soil with an emphatic 6–1 win in the first leg. A 2–1 defeat in Cairo proved more than enough to complete the formalities.

Now it is time for Ghana to once again prove they are a force on the world stage once more and their performances in 2006 and 2010 mean there is little chance of them being under-estimated by opponents.

In 2006 they beat the Czech Republic and the United States before falling to Brazil in the round of 16, while an opening win against Serbia helped them qualify from their group in 2010.

Many neutrals would like to see them advance again and help ease the pain of South Africa.

ONES TO WATCH

EMMANUEL AGYEMANG BADU
BORN: 2 December 1990
CLUB: Udinese (Italy)

Despite being only 23 years old, the midfielder is no stranger to life in the Black Stars side with more than 40 international caps to his name since making his debut in 2008.

He scored the winning penalty for Ghana as they beat Brazil in the 2009 U–20 World Cup final before agreeing to join Italian side Udinese.

KEVIN-PRINCE BOATENG
BORN: 6 March 1987
CLUB: Schalke 04 (Germany)

Kevin-Prince Boateng is vastly experienced in European football after spells with Hertha BSC, Tottenham, Borussia Dortmund, Portsmouth and Schalke. The midfielder was part of the squad at the 2010 FIFA World Cup finals and made history when he was on the opposite side to his half-brother Jerome, who plays for Germany.

GROUP G

UNITED STATES

FIFA WORLD CUP
Brasil

THE STARS AND STRIPES

The USA's best finish at the FIFA World Cup finals was their run to the semi-finals in the first edition of the competition in 1930 but they will head to Brazil with as much optimism as ever before, taking with them a squad brimming with international football experience.

COACH

JURGEN KLINSMANN

Jurgen Klinsmann is aiming to join an elite group of men who have both played in, and managed, a FIFA World Cup-winning team.

Having missed out on that achievement while managing Germany during the 2006 FIFA World Cup, the 49-year-old will be looking to match the efforts of Mario Zagallo (Brazil) and Franz Beckenbauer (West Germany) this time around.

Despite enduring a difficult start to his reign as USA manager, Klinsmann has silenced his critics in guiding the Stars and Stripes to victory over teams such as Italy, Germany and Mexico and should arrive in Brazil with a squad full of confidence.

The USA have enjoyed relative success at the FIFA World Cup in recent years, reaching the quarter-finals in 2002 before finishing top of the group ahead of England in 2010, but the Stars and Stripes will be looking to build on those recent achievements when they land on Brazilian shores.

Stars such as Tim Howard, Jermaine Jones, Landon Donovan, Clint Dempsey, Jozy Altidore and Michael Bradley have become well-known names in world football after spending significant portions of their careers playing for some of Europe's major clubs including Tottenham Hotspur, Roma, Bayern Munich and Everton. Those players' level of experience at the highest level, mixed with the relative youth of newcomers such as Joe Corona and Mikkel Diskerud, will no doubt prove pivotal if the USA are to progress from the group stage and beyond in Brazil.

In Jurgen Klinsmann, they have a manager who has experienced great success in world football as a player, winning the UEFA Cup, Bundesliga, German Footballer of the Year and FIFA World Cup in a glittering career.

If the former Inter Milan and Bayern Munich forward is to guide his team of players to success in Brazil, however, it will no doubt rank as his biggest achievement of all time, elevating him into American soccer folklore.

Above: The United States line up before the qualifying win over Mexico in Columbus, Ohio.

STAR MAN

CLINT DEMPSEY

BORN: 9 March 1983
CLUB: Seattle Sounders (USA)
Former Tottenham and Fulham forward Clint Dempsey is no stranger to playing at the highest level, having spent six years plying his trade in the English Premier League, becoming the all-time highest scoring American on English shores.

He returned to his native homeland with Seattle Sounders in the summer of 2013 to further enhance his profile back home, and his partnership with fellow striker Landon Donovan could prove key to his country's success in Brazil.

Dempsey will be looking to add to his impressive FIFA World Cup finals goal tally, having scored in two previous competitions.

The USA enjoyed arguably their biggest footballing success of recent times when they reached the final of the FIFA Confederations Cup in 2009, eventually throwing away a two-goal lead to lose 3–2 to Brazil in South Africa.

Memorably, they also beat the eventual world champions, Spain, in their semi-final thanks to goals from Altidore and Dempsey in a result which forced the world of football to really sit up and take notice.

Many of the players who played their part in that tournament could feature in Klinsmann's 23-man squad in Brazil, again highlighting the level of experience the German coach will have at his disposal.

Qualifying for the 2014 FIFA World Cup was a relatively straightforward affair for the men in red, white and blue, finishing top of their CONCACAF groups in both rounds with 11 wins from their 16 matches.

Klinsmann's team sealed a place in Brazil with two games to spare following a 2–0 victory over Mexico at the Columbus Crew Stadium in September 2013 thanks to goals from Eddie Johnson and Donovan and, in doing so, scuppered their fierce rivals' chances of automatic qualification.

Dempsey finished the campaign as top scorer with an impressive seven goals in 13 appearances but his team will need to avoid slip-ups such as those against Jamaica and Costa Rica during qualifying if they are to do well in Brazil.

That said, Klinsmann's team finished strongly, losing only one of their last nine competitive matches – a disappointing 3–1 defeat by fellow qualifiers Costa Rica – and the German boss will be encouraged by the six clean sheets kept during that run as he prepares his team for a much tougher test in Brazil.

ONES TO WATCH

LANDON DONOVAN

BORN: 4 March 1982
CLUB: LA Galaxy (USA)
Landon Donovan is no stranger to the FIFA World Cup finals, having appeared at the last three editions.

Far and away his country's leading all-time goalscorer with more than 50 to his name, the former Everton and Bayern Munich forward will be hoping to score at a third FIFA World Cup after finding the net in Korea Republic and Japan and then South Africa.

TIM HOWARD

BORN: 6 March 1979
CLUB: Everton (England)
The experienced goalkeeper has won almost a century of caps for his country and has spent over a decade playing at the highest level of English football with Manchester United and then Everton, the New Jersey native becoming one of the Premier League's most reliable keepers.

He was an unused substitute at the 2006 FIFA World Cup finals but played every minute of their 2010 campaign.

BELGIUM

FIFA WORLD CUP Brasil

RED DEVILS

Belgium have perhaps generated the biggest buzz of Europe's 13 qualifiers as Marc Wilmots heads to Brazil with a squad comprising some of the brightest talents in the game. Having reached the round of 16 the last time they qualified in 2002, they are widely tipped to go further this time.

COACH

MARC WILMOTS

As a player, Marc Wilmots scored the goal which secured Belgium's qualification for the 2002 FIFA World Cup and he holds the distinction of being the last Belgian to score in a Finals against Russia.

Now, after a brief spell as a politician and a forgettable stint in club management, Wilmots finds himself in charge of his country's national team. He stepped up in May 2012, having served as assistant to Dick Advocaat and then Georges Leekens, and eased a talented squad through qualification. Wilmots has yet to taste defeat in a competitive game as Belgium coach, overseeing eight wins and two draws in 10 matches.

Belgium hailed a 'golden generation' as they reached the semi-finals of the 1986 FIFA World Cup finals but the class of 2014 have every chance of eclipsing that achievement.

National heroes of 28 years ago such as Jean-Marie Pfaff, Jan Ceulemans and Enzo Scifo could be joined in the hall of fame by modern-day counterparts Thibaut Courtois, Marouane Fellaini and Eden Hazard if they fulfil their undoubted potential.

Led by former midfielder Marc Wilmots – Belgium's leading FIFA World Cup goalscorer – the majority of the current squad ply their trade in Europe's top leagues.

England's Premier League is home to 12 of the 22 players used by Wilmots in their qualifying campaign, with Chelsea and Tottenham the main two clubs reaping the rewards. Kevin De Bruyne may not have been a regular starter at Stamford Bridge in 2013–14 but the baby-faced winger was Belgium's leading scorer with four goals, albeit most of them coming while he was enjoying a loan spell at German side Werder Bremen.

Courtois and powerful young striker Romelu Lukaku have also found themselves loaned out by the Blues, with the latter shooting to prominence after scoring 17 goals for West Bromwich Albion during the 2012–13 season, including a hat-trick against Manchester United.

Lukaku, who cost Chelsea £18million from Anderlecht in 2011, has spent the last campaign at Everton, where he further enhanced his reputation with a number of match-winning displays.

Playmaker Hazard completes Chelsea's Belgian contingent, while

Above: The Belgium team lines up before their qualifying game against Wales.

STAR MAN

VINCENT KOMPANY

BORN: 10 April 1986
CLUB: Manchester City (England)
Belgium only conceded four goals in their 10 qualifying matches and that was largely down to skipper Vincent Kompany.

The Manchester City centre-back, equally influential at club level, also has goals in his game, scoring twice in Belgium's qualifying campaign. His dedication is never in doubt and was witnessed against Serbia when he collided with goalkeeper Vladimir Stojkovic and required lengthy treatment. He played on for an hour with what turned out to be a broken nose, cracked eye socket and mild concussion.

Spurs can call on three players; defender Jan Vertonghen, central midfielder Moussa Dembele and winger Nacer Chadli.

Guillaume Gillet (Anderlecht) and Ilombe Mboyo (Genk) were the only Belgian-based players used in qualifying by Wilmots.

Lukaku, whose two goals against Croatia secured qualification, was only nine years old when his country last competed in a major tournament, the 2002 FIFA World Cup in Korea/Japan.

"I was in the third grade," he said. "I remember we played against Brazil and we were allowed to watch the match at school."

Belgium progressed from the group stages after finishing second to hosts Japan but that resulted in a round-of-16 clash with the eventual winners, with Rivaldo and Ronaldo scoring second-half goals.

In qualifying for the 2014 FIFA World Cup, Belgium topped Group A with 26 points. Defensive duo Vincent Kompany and Vertonghen got Wilmots' side up and running in Cardiff, scoring the goals in a comfortable 2–0 victory over Wales, and after drawing with

Croatia, it was a 3–0 win in Serbia which really highlighted the talent in Belgium's squad. Christian Benteke headed the opening goal and De Bruyne doubled their advantage with a neat finish midway through the second half. Kevin Mirallas' breakaway third capped a fine display and moved Belgium to the top of Group A – a position they never relinquished.

Wins against Scotland, Macedonia twice in quick

succession, Serbia and Scotland followed before the trip to Zagreb which would secure their place in Brazil and further boost Lukaku's profile.

Following the Croatia victory, a jubilant Wilmots said: "The story is not over by far. I will keep on working and preparing. It is now up to me and my staff to get this team in the best possible condition. Belgium have been given back their fans and their soul. If anyone should be congratulated for that, it must be the players as they are the ones that have performed."

A disappointing draw with Wales closed the group, but by that stage there had been plenty of signs that the young team from the Low Countries can end the 2014 FIFA World Cup on a high.

ONES TO WATCH

CHRISTIAN BENTEKE

(Christian Benteke Liolo)
BORN: 3 December 1990
CLUB: Aston Villa (England)
Since joining Aston Villa from Genk in August 2012, powerhouse Christian Benteke has become one of the most feared strikers in Europe. Scoring 19 goals in his debut season in the English Premier League in 2012–13 was no mean feat and he continued his impressive form during the following campaign.

EDEN HAZARD

BORN: 7 January 1991
CLUB: Chelsea (England)
Eden Hazard joined Chelsea from French club Lille for a staggering £32million in June 2012. After scoring 13 goals in all competitions in his first season, the diminutive playmaker found himself nominated for the illustrious Ballon d'Or. He scored two goals in qualifying, the second being a vital winner against Macedonia.

ALGERIA

FIFA WORLD CUP Brasil

DESERT FOXES

The only country to qualify from North Africa, Algeria are no strangers to pulling off shock results at FIFA World Cup competitions and this proud and passionate football-mad nation will again be looking to take on the role of giantkillers in South America.

COACH

VAHID HALILHODZIC

After being capped 15 times by Yugoslavia in his playing days, Vahid Halilhodzic has carved out a long and successful career in management by adapting to varying circumstances with diligence and determination.

Impressive stints with Raja Casablanca and Lille helped him land a top job at club level with Paris Saint-Germain and his first international posting led to a two-year unbeaten run for Ivory Coast before an acrimonious parting of the ways with The Elephants.

Since taking charge of Algeria, the 61-year-old has shown his strength of character by casting aside several proven but ageing performers in favour of building a new team high on spirit and unity.

Algeria enjoyed a rather fortuitous passage to Brazil 2014 when edging out Burkina Faso via the away-goals rule in a play-off but nobody will ever deny the Desert Foxes a bit of FIFA World Cup luck after the injustice of their finals debut back in 1982.

The African side caused one of the tournament's biggest ever upsets when starting the group stage with a 2–1 defeat of West Germany in Spain 32 years ago, with the great Lakhdar Belloumi bagging the winning goal.

After losing to Austria, Algeria then looked to have given themselves a major chance of reaching the knockout rounds when holding on to beat Chile 3–2, having led 3–0 at half-time. However, when West Germany and Austria met in the pool's closing match a day later, they knew a narrow victory for the former would allow both teams to progress and after *Die Mannschaft* went ahead early on, each side seemed to down tools and did not try to score any more goals.

The incident inspired FIFA to ensure the final two fixtures in each group would be played simultaneously in future competitions, but veteran Algeria supporters have not forgotten or forgiven events of that summer.

Four years later, the Desert Foxes managed to draw 1–1 with Northern Ireland but bowed out following

Left to right: Algeria: (top row) Mohamed Zemmamouche, Faouzi Ghoulam, Mehdi Mostefa-Sbaa, Carl Medjani, Islam Slimani, Madjid Bougherra; (bottom row) El Arbi Soudani, Nacer Khoualed, Sofiane Feghouli, Medhi Lacen, Yacine Brahimi.

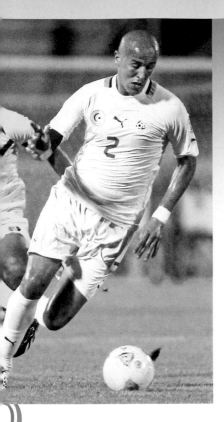

STAR MAN

MADJID BOUGHERRA

BORN: 7 October 1982
CLUB: Lekhwiya (Qatar)

Although born and raised in France, Madjid Bougherra qualifies to play for Algeria through his grandfather and the tall centre-half has been a stalwart in defence for the Desert Foxes.

A tough and uncompromising character, he impressed with several English clubs before being a big hit with Scottish club Rangers and then helping Lekhwiya win the Qatar Stars League. He does not score often but has netted important goals, including a last-minute equaliser which allowed Algeria to beat Ivory Coast in extra time at the CAF Africa Cup of Nations and the crucial strike in their FIFA World Cup play-off win over Burkina Faso.

losses to Brazil and Spain, and after failing to qualify for the next five finals they also only picked up one point at South Africa 2010.

That goalless draw with England in Cape Town did spark wild celebrations back home and among Algerian communities the world over, though, to once again demonstrate just how passionate football fans are in North Africa.

More recent evidence of the fervour created by supporters of the Desert Foxes came when the Stade Mustapha Tchaker was packed out fully six hours before kick-off when they played Burkina Faso in the second leg of their qualifying play-off.

Algeria trailed 3–2 from a tricky trip to Ouagadougou the previous week, but a run of 16 wins and three draws from the last 19 games at their Blida fortress gave hope of Vahid Halilhodzic's side turning things around.

In the end, a scrambled effort from veteran defender Madjid Bougherra helped Algeria secure a nervous 1–0 win on the night and progress to their fourth FIFA World Cup finals on the away-goals rule.

A physically imposing rearguard had been the key to their earlier group-stage success, conceding just four goals in six games against Mali, Benin and Rwanda.

For their Bosnian coach Halilhodzic, 2014 FIFA World Cup Brazil represents a chance for redemption after he was harshly sacked by Ivory Coast four months before 2010 FIFA World Cup South Africa despite masterminding their qualifying campaign, with his dismissal ironically brought on by a loss to Algeria in the CAF Africa Cup of Nations quarter-finals.

The former Paris Saint-Germain and Dinamo Zagreb boss is clearly still hurt by being denied the opportunity to compete at the highest level four years ago, but can now finally exorcise those demons in Brazil.

"Since taking over Algeria, I have worked without talking too much because it is the work that pays – I try to talk less and work more," he declared. "We have achieved something great. It is not every day you can qualify for a global competition and in particular one that is held in Brazil. It is the greatest moment of my life."

It will be a tall order for North Africa's sole representative to reach the latter stages but do not be shocked if they spring a surprise or two in the act of trying.

ONES TO WATCH

SOFIANE FEGHOULI

BORN: 26 December 1989
CLUB: Valencia (Spain)

After representing France at U–21 level and being hailed as "the new Zidane", Sofiane Feghouli slipped off *Les Bleus'* radar when joining Valencia and switched his allegiance to Algeria. He scored three times in FIFA World Cup qualifiers but is better known for creating goalscoring chances.

ISLAM SLIMANI

BORN: 18 June 1988
CLUB: Sporting Lisbon (Portugal)

A powerfully-built frontman, Islam Slimani emerged as Algeria's most potent attacking weapon when scoring five goals in the qualifying campaign, forging a good partnership with El Arabi Soudani. He moved from CR Belouizdad to Sporting Lisbon to aid his progress and looks sure to pose problems.

RUSSIA

SBORNAJA

Russia will have an even bigger incentive than most other countries to do well in Brazil as they seek to build momentum before staging the next FIFA World Cup finals themselves in 2018. Can they earn the right to become the first team to host the tournament as holders of the trophy?

COACH

FABIO CAPELLO

Few managers in history have built up as impressive a managerial record as Fabio Capello at club level, with every team he has coached winning their domestic league title at some point under his care.

AC Milan, Real Madrid, Roma and Juventus all flourished with the strict disciplinarian in charge, with Capello never afraid to sacrifice his own popularity by making tough decisions which he thought would benefit the team.

That policy led to problems during his reign in England but he still managed a win ratio of more than 66 per cent with England and is not far short of that since switching to Russia.

Fabio Capello was a man on a mission when taking charge of Russia after an unhappy end to his reign as England manager and has channelled that energy into building a tight-knit unit.

"After I had finished working in England, I was angry, and I wanted to continue working," he said on his appointment in July 2012. "I'll try to get my philosophy to match that which has brought the Russian national team success – and we will go to the World Cup in Brazil."

The Italian veteran proved true to his word as Russia edged out Portugal by a point at the top of their qualifying group, despite a nervous period where they lost to their main rivals and Northern Ireland in successive games. Conceding only five goals in 10 fixtures was key to their progress and highlighted Capello's belief that successful sides must now defend and attack in numbers to combat modern tactics.

"I think it's a little absurd that people still talk about 4-3-3, 4-4-2 and all that," he declared. "To my mind, the modern formation is 9-1. You've got nine who defend and nine who attack. You need to have a block of players, even when you're on the attack.

"You can't have a team occupying an area of 40 or 50 metres. You just don't see that any more. These days you have to be compact, with everyone in a maximum of 20 or 30 metres."

Russia's long-standing trait of being able to produce players with strong technical skills and natural

Left to right: Russia: (top row) Alexander Kokorin, Alexey Kozlov, Vasili Berezutskiy, Sergey Ignashevich, Igor Akinfeev, Roman Shirokov; (bottom row) Victor Fayzulin, Dmitry Kombarov, Denis Glushakov, Alexander Kerzhakov, Alexander Samedov.

STAR MAN

ALEXANDER KERZHAKOV

BORN: 27 November 1982
CLUB: Zenit St Petersburg (Russia)

The top scorer in Russian Premier League history with more than 200 goals, Alexander Kerzhakov has blossomed at international level under Fabio Capello.

His two spells with Zenit St Petersburg were punctuated by successful stints at Sevilla and Dynamo Moscow, but Kerzhakov is clearly enjoying life back home.

With a style of play likened to Wayne Rooney's, this tournament could come at the ideal time for the lethal 31-year-old finisher, who will also have the benefit of linking up with Zenit team-mates Roman Shirokov and Viktor Fayzulin when Russia look to get forward.

athletic ability certainly lends itself to Capello's heavy emphasis on a disciplined approach to the game.

Fourth place in 1966 may be their best finish, but under the old Soviet Union banner they regularly qualified for and acquitted themselves well at FIFA World Cup finals between 1958 and 2002.

Although failing to reach the last two tournaments, Russia built on a proud record at the European Championships during that period, making the semi-finals in 2008, having previously secured one win and three runner-up placings in the early years of that competition.

After succeeding Dutch pair Guus Hiddink and Dick Advocaat, Capello was not afraid to shake thinks up by dropping ageing stars such as Andrei Arshavin, Roman Pavlyuchenko and Pavel Pogrebnyak, but he still has a wealth of experience in his squad.

Sergey Ignashevich is closing in on a century of international appearances, while the likes of Alexander Anyukov, Alexander Kerzhakov, Vasili Berezutskiy and goalkeeper Igor Akinfeev are

not too far behind. Kerzhakov, Alexander Kokorin, Victor Fayzulin and captain Roman Shirokov all scored well in qualifying, while Alan Dzagoev was among the Golden Boot winners at UEFA EURO 2012, giving Russia balance going forward, and Capello far from reliant on one source for goals.

"I've always liked to have a lot of attacking players, though it has

to be said that doesn't necessarily mean you're going to win lots of games," joked Capello, recalling his time as Real Madrid coach.

The Italian, who will celebrate his 68th birthday during Brazil 2014, believes reaching the quarter-finals is a realistic aim for Russia – and says beyond that the margins between advancing and going out are finer than ever before.

"I think the game has really opened up," he said. "The fact you can study how the game is played all over the world has given coaches the chance to inform themselves and play a very tactical game."

Few countries will benefit from a more comprehensive preparation as Russia bid to continue their rise back up the rankings.

ONES TO WATCH

ALEXANDER KOKORIN

BORN: 19 March 1991
CLUB: Dynamo Moscow (Russia)

Big things have been expected of Alexander Kokorin ever since he scored on his debut for Dynamo Moscow as a 17-year-old and he has continued to develop into a gifted playmaker.

The collapse of last summer's 19million euros move to Zenit St Petersburg did not affect his progress and more potential suitors will surely be monitoring him in Brazil.

IGOR AKINFEEV

BORN: 8 April 1986
CLUB: CSKA Moscow (Russia)

Russia have a proud tradition of producing highly-rated goalkeepers, with the legendary Lev Yashin setting the standard, and Igor Akinfeev has established himself as the best of the current generation.

He has been the first choice at CSKA Moscow since the age of 17, winning four league titles, and made his international debut just a year later.

KOREA REPUBLIC

THE TAEGUK WARRIORS

Korea Republic had a tough battle to qualify but national hero Hong Myungbo, who coached the men's Olympic Games team to bronze at London 2012, has since taken over as head coach and will lead the side in Brazil, where he hopes to spark another run to the knockout stages.

COACH

HONG MYUNGBO

The 45-year-old is Korea Republic's most-capped player and captained the side to a best finish of fourth at the 2002 FIFA World Cup, becoming the first Asian player to play in four consecutive finals.

After retiring from playing, Hong turned to coaching and had success with Korea Republic's U-20 and U-23 sides, leading them to their best finishes in the FIFA U-20 World Cup and Olympic Games respectively. He spent the first half of 2013 as a coach at Anzhi Makhachkala under former Korea Republic head coach Guus Hiddink.

Korea Republic legend Hong Myungbo will lead the next generation of his country's players in the FIFA World Cup.

The former defender, who captained the country to their best-ever finish of fourth in the 2002 event they co-hosted with Japan, replaced Choi Kanghee as head coach following the qualification campaign.

The Taeguk Warriors' road to Brazil had a few problems along the way. Round three was negotiated relatively comfortably, with four wins from six, but in an incredibly close final group, draws in both games against Uzbekistan and a defeat in Iran left Korea Republic needing a point in their final game – at home to Iran – to secure qualification.

A 1–0 defeat left them in danger of being forced into a play-off and that would have been their fate had Uzbekistan found one more goal in their 5–1 victory over Qatar. Instead, they progressed by the slimmest of goal-difference margins and Choi stepped down from his role.

Hong was installed, with his managerial CV showing his Olympic exploits and a run to the 2009 FIFA U-20 World Cup quarter-finals in Egypt.

His generation, which included the likes of Park Jisung, Lee Woon-Jae and Lee Young-Pyo, had raised expectation levels in the nation with their performances in 2002. Since then, though, Korea Republic

Above: Korea Republic line up beofre the qualifier against Uzbekistan in Seoul.

STAR MAN

SON HEUNG MIN

BORN: 8 July 1992
CLUB: Bayer Leverkusen (Germany)

The versatile Son Heung Min was a revelation for Hamburg during the 2012–13 season, scoring 12 goals, and was linked with a host of Europe's leading clubs during last summer's transfer window.

He decided to stay in Germany, moving to Bayer Leverkusen, and featured in their UEFA Champions League campaign.

A skilful forward with an eye for goal, he tends to drift in from wide positions. He will have a lot of pressure on his young shoulders as Korea Republic fans look to him for inspiration, but his performances in the Bundesliga hint that he is up to the challenge.

KOREA REPUBLIC AT THE FIFA WORLD CUP™

1954	1st round
1986	1st round
1990	1st round
1994	1st round
1998	1st round
2002	4th place
2006	1st round
2010	Round of 16

have managed only a group-stage knockout and a last-16 appearance, while they remain without an Asian Cup success since 1960 and have finished third in the last two competitions.

Hong's task is to mould the youthful team at his disposal into one capable of going beyond the last 16 in the FIFA World Cup. To do this, the 45-year-old wants his side to embrace their strengths, focusing on counter-attacking with pace and a tight defence.

"They must remember one of the strengths of South Korean football has been the high speed," he said. "If we can capitalise on that as we go on counter-attacks, it could really work to our advantage.

"Defensive organisation is really important. It can help teams beat anybody. You shouldn't worry about whether you're playing Spain, Germany or Italy. You have to concentrate on defence and consciously maintain that focus throughout the game."

The core of his squad play their club football in Asia, with a few exports appearing in the English and German leagues. Defender

Hong Jeong Ho was the latest Korean player to make the switch to the German Bundesliga, leaving Jeju United for FC Augsburg in September.

The centre-back offers a physical presence at the heart of the Korea Republic defence and will be looking to make a name for himself on the world stage having missed the 2012 Olympics through injury.

In midfield, Hong will turn to Swansea City's Ki Sungyueng to offer protection to the back four and start attacks of their own. The 25-year-old spent the last season on loan at Sunderland having fallen out of favour with Michael Laudrup's Swans and the extra game time should ensure he is ready to play a leading role for the Taeguk Warriors in Brazil.

Further forward, the likes of Bayer Leverkusen attacker Son Heung Min, versatile Wolfsburg winger Koo Jacheol and Cardiff City midfielder Kim Bokyung will be looked upon to create chances.

Hong will also hope strikers Park Chuyoung and Ji Dongwon arrive at the finals in good form and can provide the goals that take Korea Republic to a third knockout appearance in four tournaments.

ONES TO WATCH

KOO JACHEOL

BORN: 27 February 1989
CLUB: Wolfsburg (Germany)

Koo, who can play anywhere in midfield, captained Korea Republic at the 2012 Olympic Games, scoring in the win against Japan that secured a bronze medal, and finished as leading scorer at the 2011 Asian Cup. A successful loan spell at FC Augsburg in 2012–13 helped him return to the Wolfsburg first team this season.

HONG JEONG HO

BORN: 12 August 1989
CLUB: FC Augsburg (Germany)

The dominant defender is viewed as the successor to coach Hong Myungbo at the heart of the Korea Republic defence. Strong in the challenge and good on the ball, Myungbo will look to build a defence around the Augsburg defender who made the switch to the Bundesliga in September from Jeju United.

FIFA WORLD CUP
Brasil

Spain midfielder Andres Iniesta scores the winning goal against the Netherlands in the 2010 FIFA World Cup final in Johannesburg.

FIFA WORLD CUP™ HISTORY

It is 84 years since the first FIFA World Cup was held in Uruguay and since then 76 national teams have featured in at least one tournament, while Brazil are the only country to have been present at each of the 19 finals. The history of the competition is packed with memorable matches and in this section can be found every result and every group table from 1930 through to 2010.

1930 URUGUAY

Hosts Uruguay followed up their victories at the 1924 and 1928 Olympic Games by winning the inaugural FIFA World Cup with a 4–2 defeat of neighbours and rivals Argentina, with the crowd for the final boosted by an estimated 30,000 Argentina fans crossing the River Plate.

Thirteen nations took part and all matches were played in capital city Montevideo. The four European nations competing travelled to South America on the same boat, picking up Brazil along the way.

Above: Uruguay fans rush onto the Estadio Centenario pitch at the final whistle after their team beat Argentina to win the inaugural FIFA World Cup.

GROUP 1

France	4	Mexico	1
Argentina	1	France	0
Chile	3	Mexico	0
Chile	1	France	0
Argentina	6	Mexico	3
Argentina	3	Chile	1

GROUP 2

Yugoslavia	2	Brazil	1
Yugoslavia	4	Bolivia	0
Brazil	4	Bolivia	0

GROUP 3

Romania	3	Peru	1
Uruguay	1	Peru	0
Uruguay	4	Romania	0

GROUP 4

USA	3	Belgium	0
USA	3	Paraguay	0
Paraguay	1	Belgium	0

SEMI-FINALS

Argentina	6	USA	1
Uruguay	6	Yugoslavia	1

FINAL – 30 July: Estadio Centenario, Montevideo

Uruguay 4 Dorado (12), Cea (57), Iriarte (68), Castro (89) **Argentina** 2 Peucelle (20), Stabile (37)
HT: 1–2. Att: 68,346. **Ref:** Langenus (Belgium)
Uruguay: Ballestrero, Gestido, Mascheroni, Castro, Scarone, Andrade, Nasazzi, Fernandez, Dorado, Cea, Iriarte.
Argentina: Botasso, Peucelle, Paternoster, Varallo, Stabile, Della Torre, J Evaristo, Monti, Ferreira, M Evaristo, Suarez.
Top scorer: 8 Stabile (Argentina)

1934 ITALY

Italy overcame a busy schedule and some bruising encounters to beat Czechoslovakia in a thrilling final, with the hosts equalising in the 81st minute of normal time before prevailing in extra time.

Holders Uruguay refused to take part as the Azzurri had pulled out of the previous tournament, while Argentina and Brazil sent weakened teams, allowing European sides to fill all eight quarter-final places.

Above: Italy's triumphant players lift coach Vittorio Pozzo shoulder-high after they beat Czechoslovakia in Rome.

PRELIMINARY ROUND

Sweden	3	Argentina	2
Austria	3	France	2 *
Germany	5	Belgium	2
Spain	3	Brazil	1
Hungary	4	Egypt	2
Switzerland	3	Netherlands	2
Italy	7	USA	1
Czechoslovakia	2	Romania	1

*After extra time

QUARTER-FINALS

Czechoslovakia	3	Switzerland	2
Germany	2	Sweden	1
Italy	1	Spain	1 *
Austria	2	Hungary	1
Italy	1	Spain	0

*After extra time

SEMI-FINALS

Italy	1	Austria	0
Czechoslovakia	3	Germany	1

THIRD-PLACE MATCH

Germany	3	Austria	2

FINAL – 10 June: Nazionale PNF, Rome

Italy 2 Orsi (81), Schiavio (95) **Czechoslovakia** 1 Puc (71) After extra time
HT: 0–0. Att: 55,000. **Ref:** Eklind (Sweden)
Italy: Combi, Schiavio, Ferraris, Guaita, Monzeglio, Ferrari, Meazza, Allemandi, Bertolini, Monti, Orsi.
Czechoslovakia: Planicka, Puc, Junek, Svoboda, Sobotka, Ctyroky, Kostalek, Zenisek, Nejedly, Krcil, Cambal.

Top scorer: 5 Nejedly (Czechoslovakia)

1938 FRANCE

Italy became the first team to successfully defend the FIFA World Cup as star striker Silvio Piola scored twice in a 4-2 final defeat of Hungary, with the victors wearing black shirts at the request of dictator Benito Mussolini in the last major sporting event before war broke out.

Top-scorer Leonidas hit a hat-trick in Brazil's 6-5 win over Poland, with Ernest Wilimowski ending up on the losing side despite netting four times in that game.

Above: Italy captain Giuseppe Meazza receives the Jules Rimet Trophy after retaining their title by beating Hungary in the final of the 1938 FIFA World Cup.

FIRST ROUND

Switzerland	1	Germany	1	*
Hungary	6	Dutch East Indies	0	
France	3	Belgium	1	
Cuba	3	Romania	3	*
Italy	2	Norway	1	*
Brazil	6	Poland	5	*
Czechoslovakia	3	Netherlands	0	*
Cuba	2	Romania	1	
Switzerland	4	Germany	2	

*After extra time

QUARTER-FINALS

Brazil	1	Czechoslovakia	1	*
Hungary	2	Switzerland	0	
Sweden	8	Cuba	0	
Italy	3	France	1	
Brazil	2	Czechoslovakia	1	

*After extra time

SEMI-FINALS

Hungary	5	Sweden	1
Italy	2	Brazil	1

THIRD-PLACE MATCH

Brazil	4	Sweden	2

FINAL – 19 June: Stade Olympique de Colombes, Paris

Italy 4   Colaussi (6, 35), Piola (16, 82)   **Hungary** 2   Titkos (8), Sarosi (70)
HT: 3-1. **Att:** 45,000. **Ref:** Capdeville (France)
Italy: Olivieri, Foni, Biavati, Colaussi, Ferrari, Meazza, Andreolo, Rava, Serantoni, Piola, Locatelli.
Hungary: Szabo, Szalay, Sas, Sarosi, Szucs, Lazar, Polgar, Zsengeller, Vincze, Titkos, Biro.

Top scorer: 7 Leonidas (Brazil)

1950 BRAZIL

Almost 200,000 spectators were left stunned at the Maracana Stadium in Rio as Uruguay came from behind to upset Brazil in what was the deciding match of this tournament.

The hosts had previously thrashed Sweden 7-1 and Spain 6-1 in a concluding four-team mini-league, but succumbed to opponents who had a draw and a narrow win from their opening games. Earlier, England suffered an embarrassing loss to the USA.

Above: Uruguay match-winner Ghiggia turns away to celebrate scoring the decisive goal against hosts Brazil in the last game of the final group to clinch their second FIFA World Cup success.

GROUP 1

Brazil	4	Mexico	0
Yugoslavia	3	Switzerland	0
Brazil	2	Switzerland	2
Yugoslavia	4	Mexico	1
Brazil	2	Yugoslavia	0
Switzerland	2	Mexico	1

	P	W	D	L	F	A	Pts
Brazil	3	2	1	0	8	2	5
Yugoslavia	3	2	0	1	7	3	4
Switzerland	3	1	1	1	4	6	3
Mexico	3	0	0	3	2	10	0

GROUP 2

England	2	Chile	0
Spain	3	USA	1
Spain	2	Chile	0
USA	1	England	0
Spain	1	England	0
Chile	5	USA	2

	P	W	D	L	F	A	Pts
Spain	3	3	0	0	6	1	6
England	3	1	0	2	2	2	2
Chile	3	1	0	2	5	6	2
USA	3	1	0	2	4	8	2

GROUP 3

Sweden	3	Italy	2
Sweden	2	Paraguay	2
Italy	2	Paraguay	0

	P	W	D	L	F	A	Pts
Sweden	2	1	1	0	5	4	3
Italy	2	1	0	1	4	3	2
Paraguay	2	0	1	1	2	4	1

GROUP 4

Uruguay	8	Bolivia	0

	P	W	D	L	F	A	Pts
Uruguay	1	1	0	0	8	0	2
Bolivia	1	0	0	1	0	8	0

Top scorer: 8 Ademir (Brazil)

FINAL GROUP

Uruguay	2	Spain	2
Brazil	7	Sweden	1
Brazil	6	Spain	1
Uruguay	3	Sweden	2
Sweden	3	Spain	1
Uruguay	2	Brazil	1

	P	W	D	L	F	A	Pts
Uruguay	3	2	1	0	7	5	5
Brazil	3	2	0	1	14	4	4
Sweden	3	1	0	2	6	11	2
Spain	3	0	1	2	4	11	1

1954 SWITZERLAND

West Germany secured a surprise success when battling back from 2-0 down to beat the Magical Magyars of Hungary 3-2 in a final dubbed the Miracle of Berne.

In a tournament which yielded the highest average of goals per game at 5.38, Ferenc Puskas had earlier helped Hungary extend their unbeaten run to 31 matches, with Sandor Kocsis scoring 11 times, while there was television coverage for the first time.

GROUP 1

Yugoslavia	1	France	0
Brazil	5	Mexico	0
Brazil	1	Yugoslavia	1 *
France	3	Mexico	2

* After extra time

	P	W	D	L	F	A	Pts
Brazil	2	1	1	0	6	1	3
Yugoslavia	2	1	1	0	2	1	3
France	2	1	0	1	3	3	2
Mexico	2	0	0	2	2	8	0

GROUP 2

Germany FR	4	Turkey	1
Hungary	9	Korea Republic	0
Hungary	8	Germany FR	3
Turkey	7	Korea Republic	0
Germany FR	7	Turkey	2 **

** Play-off

	P	W	D	L	F	A	Pts
Hungary	2	2	0	0	17	3	4
Germany FR	3	2	0	1	14	11	4
Turkey	3	1	0	2	10	11	2
Korea Rep	2	0	0	2	0	16	0

GROUP 3

Austria	1	Scotland	0
Uruguay	2	Czechoslovakia	0
Uruguay	7	Scotland	0
Austria	5	Czechoslovakia	0

	P	W	D	L	F	A	Pts
Uruguay	2	2	0	0	9	0	4
Austria	2	2	0	0	6	0	4
Czechoslovakia	2	0	0	2	0	7	0
Scotland	2	0	0	2	0	8	0

GROUP 4

Switzerland	2	Italy	1
England	4	Belgium	4 *
Italy	4	Belgium	1
England	2	Switzerland	0
Switzerland	4	Italy	1 **

* After extra time ** Play-off

	P	W	D	L	F	A	Pts
Switzerland	3	2	0	1	6	4	4
England	2	1	1	0	6	4	3
Italy	3	1	0	2	6	7	2
Belgium	2	0	1	1	5	8	1

QUARTER-FINALS

Austria	7	Switzerland	5
Uruguay	4	England	2
Hungary	4	Brazil	2
Germany FR	2	Yugoslavia	0

SEMI-FINALS

Hungary	4	Uruguay	2 *
Germany FR	6	Austria	1

* After extra time

THIRD-PLACE MATCH

Austria	3	Uruguay	1

FINAL – 4 July: Wankdorf Stadium, Berne

Germany FR 3 Morlock (10), Rahn (18, 84) **Hungary** 2 Puskas (6), Czibor (8)
HT: 2-2. Att: 62,500. **Ref:** Ling (England)
Germany FR: Turek, Kohlmeyer, Eckel, Posipal, Mai, Liebrich, Rahn, Morlock, O Walter, F Walter, Schaefer.
Hungary: Grosics, Buzanszky, Lorant, Lantos, Bozsik, Zakarias, Kocsis, Hidegkuti, Puskas, Czibor, Toth.
Top scorer: 11 Kocsis (Hungary)

1958 SWEDEN

Brazil began their love affair with the FIFA World Cup, with a 17-year-old Pele scoring twice in their 5-2 win over hosts Sweden in the decider – which remains the sole triumph for a South American team in Europe.

All four British nations featured for the only time, with Northern Ireland and Wales reaching the quarter-finals, while France forward Just Fontaine scored a record 13 goals to help Les Bleus finish third.

GROUP 1

Germany FR	3	Argentina	1
Northern Ireland	1	Czechoslovakia	0
Argentina	3	Northern Ireland	1
Germany FR	2	Czechoslovakia	2
Czechoslovakia	6	Argentina	1
Germany FR	2	Northern Ireland	2
Northern Ireland	2	Czechoslovakia	1 **

** Play-off

	P	W	D	L	F	A	Pts
N Ireland	4	2	1	1	6	6	5
Germany FR	3	1	2	0	7	5	4
Czechoslovakia	4	1	1	2	9	6	3
Argentina	3	1	0	2	5	10	2

GROUP 2

Yugoslavia	1	Scotland	1
France	7	Paraguay	3
Yugoslavia	3	France	2
Paraguay	3	Scotland	2
Paraguay	3	Yugoslavia	3
France	2	Scotland	1

	P	W	D	L	F	A	Pts
France	3	2	0	1	11	7	4
Yugoslavia	3	1	2	0	7	6	4
Paraguay	3	1	1	1	9	12	3
Scotland	3	0	1	2	4	6	1

GROUP 3

Sweden	3	Mexico	0
Hungary	1	Wales	1
Mexico	1	Wales	1
Sweden	2	Hungary	1
Sweden	0	Wales	0
Hungary	4	Mexico	0
Wales	2	Hungary	1 **

** Play-off

	P	W	D	L	F	A	Pts
Sweden	3	2	1	0	5	1	5
Wales	4	1	3	0	4	3	5
Hungary	4	1	1	2	7	5	3
Mexico	3	0	1	2	1	8	1

GROUP 4

Soviet Union	2	England	2
Brazil	3	Austria	0
Soviet Union	2	Austria	0
Brazil	0	England	0
Brazil	2	Soviet Union	0
England	2	Austria	2
Soviet Union	1	England	0 **

** Play-off

	P	W	D	L	F	A	Pts
Brazil	3	2	1	0	5	0	5
Soviet Union	4	2	1	1	5	4	5
England	4	0	3	1	4	5	3
Austria	3	0	1	2	2	7	1

QUARTER-FINALS

Brazil	1	Wales	0
France	4	N Ireland	0
Germany FR	1	Yugoslavia	0
Sweden	2	Soviet Union	0

SEMI-FINALS

Sweden	3	Germany FR	1
Brazil	5	France	2

THIRD-PLACE MATCH

France	6	Germany FR	3

FINAL – 29 June: Rasunda Stadium, Solna

Brazil 5 Vava (9, 32), Pele (55, 90), Zagallo (68) **Sweden** 2 Liedholm (4), Simonsson (80)
HT: 2-1. Att: 49,737. **Ref:** Guigue (France)
Brazil: Gilmar, Bellini, Djalma Santos, Didi, Zagallo, Pele, Garrincha, Nilton Santos, Orlando, Zito, Vava.
Sweden: Svensson, Bergmark, Axbom, Liedholm, Parling, Hamrin, Gren, Simonsson, Skoglund, Gustavsson, Borjesson.
Top scorer: 13 Fontaine (France)

1962 CHILE

Brazil lost Pele early on to a hamstring injury but another of the greats, Garrincha, turned in a series of superb displays to help them cope with his absence, with the 'Little Bird' leading the defending champions all the way to a final defeat of Czechoslovakia.

The tournament is less fondly remembered for the Battle of Santiago, with two players sent off in a match between Chile and Italy which was littered with fouls and altercations.

GROUP 1

Uruguay	2	Colombia	1
Soviet Union	2	Yugoslavia	0
Yugoslavia	3	Uruguay	1
Soviet Union	4	Colombia	4
Soviet Union	2	Uruguay	1
Yugoslavia	5	Colombia	0

	P	W	D	L	F	A	Pts
Soviet Union	3	2	1	0	8	5	5
Yugoslavia	3	2	0	1	8	3	4
Uruguay	3	1	0	2	4	6	2
Colombia	3	0	1	2	5	11	1

GROUP 2

Chile	3	Switzerland	1
Germany FR	0	Italy	0
Chile	2	Italy	0
Germany FR	2	Switzerland	1
Germany FR	2	Chile	0
Italy	3	Switzerland	0

	P	W	D	L	F	A	Pts
Germany FR	3	2	1	0	4	1	5
Chile	3	2	0	1	5	3	4
Italy	3	1	1	1	3	2	3
Switzerland	3	0	0	3	2	8	0

GROUP 3

Brazil	2	Mexico	0
Czechoslovakia	1	Spain	0
Brazil	0	Czechoslovakia	0
Spain	1	Mexico	0
Brazil	2	Spain	1
Mexico	3	Czechoslovakia	1

	P	W	D	L	F	A	Pts
Brazil	3	2	1	0	4	1	5
Czechoslovakia	3	1	1	1	1	3	3
Mexico	3	1	0	2	3	4	2
Spain	3	1	0	2	2	3	2

GROUP 4

Argentina	1	Bulgaria	0
Hungary	2	England	1
England	3	Argentina	1
Hungary	6	Bulgaria	1
Hungary	0	Argentina	0
England	0	Bulgaria	0

	P	W	D	L	F	A	Pts
Hungary	3	2	1	0	8	2	5
England	3	1	1	1	4	3	3
Argentina	3	1	1	1	2	3	3
Bulgaria	3	0	1	2	1	7	1

QUARTER-FINALS

Chile	2	Soviet Union	1
Yugoslavia	1	Germany FR	0
Brazil	3	England	1
Czechoslovakia	1	Hungary	0

SEMI-FINALS

Brazil	4	Chile	2
Czechoslovakia	3	Yugoslavia	1

THIRD-PLACE MATCH

Chile	1	Yugoslavia	0

FINAL – 17 June: Estadio Nacional, Santiago

Brazil 3 Amarildo (17), Zito (69), Vava (78) **Czechoslovakia 1** Masopust (15)
HT: 1–1. Att: 107,412. Ref: Gloeckner (German DR)
Brazil: Gilmar, Djalma Santos, Mauro Ramos, Zito, Zozimo, Nilton Santos, Garrincha, Didi, Vava, Amarildo, Zagallo.
Czecholslovakia: Schrojf, Popluhar, Novak, Pluskal, Masopust, Scherer, Jelinek, Tichy, Pospichal, Kadraba, Kvasnak.
Top scorer: 4 Garrincha (Brazil), Vava (Brazil), Sanchez (Chile), Jerkovic (Yugoslavia), Albert (Hungary), Ivanov (Soviet Union)

1966 ENGLAND

England capitalised on home advantage as Geoff Hurst's hat-trick helped them upset favourites West Germany with a 4–2 win in a final best remembered for the controversy over whether his second strike crossed the line.

An average of 51,000 fans saw each match and Portugal star Eusebio was the player of the tournament with nine goals, including four in a 5–3 quarter-final defeat of Korea DPR, who had led 3–0 after previously knocking out Italy.

GROUP 1

England	0	Uruguay	0
France	1	Mexico	1
Uruguay	2	France	1
England	2	Mexico	0
Uruguay	0	Mexico	0
England	2	France	0

	P	W	D	L	F	A	Pts
England	3	2	1	0	4	0	5
Uruguay	3	1	2	0	2	1	4
Mexico	3	0	2	1	1	3	2
France	3	0	1	2	2	5	1

GROUP 2

Germany FR	5	Switzerland	0
Argentina	2	Spain	1
Spain	2	Switzerland	1
Germany FR	0	Argentina	0
Argentina	2	Switzerland	0
Germany FR	2	Spain	1

	P	W	D	L	F	A	Pts
Germany FR	3	2	1	0	7	1	5
Argentina	3	2	1	0	4	1	5
Spain	3	1	0	2	4	5	2
Switzerland	3	0	0	3	1	9	0

GROUP 3

Brazil	2	Bulgaria	0
Portugal	3	Hungary	1
Hungary	3	Brazil	1
Portugal	3	Bulgaria	0
Portugal	3	Brazil	1
Hungary	3	Bulgaria	1

	P	W	D	L	F	A	Pts
Portugal	3	3	0	0	9	2	6
Hungary	3	2	0	1	7	5	4
Brazil	3	1	0	2	4	6	2
Bulgaria	3	0	0	3	1	8	0

GROUP 4

Soviet Union	3	Korea DPR	0
Italy	2	Chile	0
Korea DPR	1	Chile	1
Soviet Union	1	Italy	0
Korea DPR	1	Italy	0
Soviet Union	2	Chile	1

	P	W	D	L	F	A	Pts
Soviet Union	3	3	0	0	6	1	6
Korea DPR	3	1	1	1	2	4	3
Italy	3	1	0	2	2	2	2
Chile	3	0	1	2	2	5	1

QUARTER-FINALS

England	1	Argentina	0
Germany FR	4	Uruguay	0
Soviet Union	2	Hungary	1
Portugal	5	Korea DPR	3

SEMI-FINALS

Germany FR	2	Soviet Union	1
England	2	Portugal	1

THIRD-PLACE MATCH

Portugal	2	Soviet Union	1

FINAL – 30 July: Wembley, London

England 4 Hurst (18, 101, 120), Peters (78) **Germany FR 2** Haller (12), Weber (89)
After extra time
HT: 1–1. Att: 96,924. Ref: Dienst (Switzerland)
England: Banks, Cohen, Wilson, Stiles, J Charlton, Moore, Ball, B Charlton, Hurst, Peters, Hunt.
Germany FR: Tilkowski, Hoettges, Schnellinger, Beckenbauer, Schulz, Weber, Haller, Seeler, Held, Emmerich, Overath.
Top scorer: 9 Eusebio (Portugal)

1970 MEXICO

Brazil earned the right to keep the Jules Rimet Trophy after Pele helped them to claim a third FIFA World Cup triumph at the first tournament staged outside Europe and South America.

Jairzinho scored in every game, while Gerson, Tostao and Rivelino also shone in an attacking line-up which followed

up a 100 per cent record in qualifying by winning six straight games in Mexico, capping off a 4–1 final defeat of Italy with a Carlos Alberto wonder goal.

Gerd Mueller top-scored with 10 for West Germany, while England goalkeeper Gordon Banks will always be remembered for an amazing save from Pele.

Above: Captain Carlos Alberto crowns Brazil's majestic progress to claiming the Jules Rimet Trophy with his side's famous fourth goal against Italy in the 1970 final.

GROUP 1

Mexico	0	Soviet Union	0
Belgium	3	El Salvador	0
Soviet Union	4	Belgium	1
Mexico	4	El Salvador	0
Soviet Union	2	El Salvador	0
Mexico	1	Belgium	0

	P	W	D	L	F	A	Pts
Soviet Union	3	2	1	0	6	1	5
Mexico	3	2	1	0	5	0	5
Belgium	3	1	0	2	4	5	2
El Salvador	3	0	0	3	0	9	0

GROUP 2

Uruguay	2	Israel	0
Italy	1	Sweden	0
Uruguay	0	Italy	0
Sweden	1	Israel	1
Sweden	1	Uruguay	0
Italy	0	Israel	0

	P	W	D	L	F	A	Pts
Italy	3	1	2	0	1	0	4
Uruguay	3	1	1	1	2	1	3
Sweden	3	1	1	1	2	2	3
Israel	3	0	2	1	1	3	2

QUARTER-FINALS

Brazil	4	Peru	2	
Germany FR	3	England	2	*
Italy	4	Mexico	1	
Uruguay	1	Soviet Union	0	*

After extra time

SEMI-FINALS

Brazil	3	Uruguay	1	
Italy	4	Germany FR	3	*

After extra time

GROUP 3

England	1	Romania	0
Brazil	4	Czechoslovakia	1
Romania	2	Czechoslovakia	1
Brazil	1	England	0
Brazil	3	Romania	2
England	1	Czechoslovakia	0

	P	W	D	L	F	A	Pts
Brazil	3	3	0	0	8	3	6
England	3	2	0	1	2	1	4
Romania	3	1	0	2	4	5	2
Czechoslovakia	3	0	0	3	2	7	0

GROUP 4

Peru	3	Bulgaria	2
Germany FR	2	Morocco	1
Peru	3	Morocco	0
Germany FR	5	Bulgaria	2
Germany FR	3	Peru	1
Bulgaria	1	Morocco	1

	P	W	D	L	F	A	Pts
Germany FR	3	3	0	0	10	4	6
Peru	3	2	0	1	7	5	4
Bulgaria	3	0	1	2	5	9	1
Morocco	3	0	1	2	2	6	1

THIRD-PLACE MATCH

Germany FR	1	Uruguay	0

FINAL – 21 June: Estadio Azteca, Mexico City
Brazil 4 Pele (18), Gerson (66), Jairzinho (71), Carlos Alberto (86) **Italy** 1 Boninsegna (37)
HT: 1–1. **Att:** 107,412. **Ref:** Gloeckner (German DR)
Brazil: Felix, Brito, Wilson Piazza, Carlos Alberto, Clodoaldo, Jairzinho, Gerson, Tostao, Pele, Rivelino, Everaldo.
Italy: Albertosi, Burgnich, Facchetti, Cera, Rosato, Bertini (Juliano 74), Riva, Domenghini, Mazzola, De Sisti, Boninsegna (Rivera 84).
Top scorer: 10 Mueller (Germany FR)

1974 WEST GERMANY

West Germany captain Franz Beckenbauer lifted the new FIFA World Cup Trophy after the hosts edged out a Johan Cruyff-inspired Dutch team which had thrilled spectators with their revolutionary brand of Total Football.

The Netherlands got off to a flying start in the Munich decider when Johan Neeskens converted the first penalty awarded in a final but Paul Breitner equalised with another spot-kick before Gerd Mueller scored the winning goal.

Poland proved a surprise package, with adidas Golden Shoe winner Grzegorz Lato netting seven times and Andrzej Szarmach five en route to third place.

Right: Frank Beckenbauer becomes the first man to lift the new FIFA World Cup Trophy after hosts West Germany beat the Netherlands in the 1974 final.

GROUP 1

Germany FR	1	Chile				0
German DR	2	Australia				0
Australia	0	Germany FR				3
Chile	1	German DR				1
Australia	0	Chile				0
German DR	0	Germany FR				0

	P	W	D	L	F	A	Pts
German DR	3	2	1	0	4	1	5
Germany FR	3	2	0	1	4	1	4
Chile	3	0	2	1	1	2	2
Australia	3	0	1	2	0	5	1

GROUP 2

Brazil	0	Yugoslavia				0
Zaire	0	Scotland				2
Scotland	0	Brazil				0
Yugoslavia	9	Zaire				0
Scotland	1	Yugoslavia				1
Zaire	0	Brazil				3

	P	W	D	L	F	A	Pts
Yugoslavia	3	1	2	0	10	1	4
Brazil	3	1	2	0	3	0	4
Scotland	3	1	2	0	3	1	4
Zaire	3	0	0	3	0	14	0

SECOND ROUND

GROUP A

Netherlands	4	Argentina				0
Brazil	1	German DR				0
Brazil	2	Argentina				1
Netherlands	2	German DR				0
Argentina	1	German DR				1
Netherlands	2	Brazil				0

	P	W	D	L	F	A	Pts
Netherlands	3	3	0	0	8	0	6
Brazil	3	2	0	1	3	3	4
German DR	3	0	1	2	1	4	1
Argentina	3	0	1	2	2	7	1

GROUP 3

Sweden	0	Bulgaria				0
Uruguay	0	Netherlands				2
Netherlands	0	Sweden				0
Bulgaria	1	Uruguay				1
Bulgaria	1	Netherlands				4
Sweden	3	Uruguay				0

	P	W	D	L	F	A	Pts
Netherlands	3	2	1	0	6	1	5
Sweden	3	1	2	0	3	0	4
Bulgaria	3	0	2	1	2	5	2
Uruguay	3	0	1	2	1	6	1

GROUP 4

Italy	3	Haiti				1
Poland	3	Argentina				2
Argentina	1	Italy				1
Poland	7	Haiti				0
Poland	2	Italy				1
Argentina	4	Haiti				1

	P	W	D	L	F	A	Pts
Poland	3	3	0	0	12	3	6
Argentina	3	1	1	1	7	5	3
Italy	3	1	1	1	5	4	3
Haiti	3	0	0	3	2	14	0

GROUP B

Germany FR	2	Yugoslavia				0
Poland	1	Sweden				0
Poland	2	Yugoslavia				1
Germany FR	4	Sweden				2
Germany FR	1	Poland				0
Sweden	2	Yugoslavia				1

	P	W	D	L	F	A	Pts
Germany FR	3	3	0	0	7	2	6
Poland	3	2	0	1	3	2	4
Sweden	3	1	0	2	4	6	2
Yugoslavia	3	0	0	3	2	6	0

THIRD-PLACE MATCH

Brazil	0	Poland	1

FINAL – 7 July: Olympic Stadium, Munich

Netherlands 1 Neeskens (2, pen) **Germany FR** 2 Breitner (25, pen), Mueller (43)
HT: 1-2. Att: 78,200. Ref: Taylor (England)
Netherlands: Jongbloed, Haan, Van Hanegem, Jansen, Krol, Neeskens, Cruyff, Rensenbrink, (R van de Kerkhof 46), Rep, Rijsbergen (De Jong 68), Suurbier.
Germany FR: Maier, Vogts, Breitner, Schwarzenbeck, Beckenbauer, Grabowski, Overath, Mueller, Hoeness, Bonhof, Hoelzenbein.
Top scorer: 7 Lato (Poland)

1978 ARGENTINA

Netherlands lost out to the host nation in the final for the second straight tournament as star striker Mario Kempes led Argentina to their first outright victory against an iconic backdrop of blue and white ticker tape thrown onto the pitch by home fans.

Argentina's 6–0 rout of a lacklustre Peru, when needing an emphatic victory to finish ahead of Brazil in the second group stage, inspired a subsequent ruling that the final round of pool matches should begin at the same time.

Tunisia claimed a first FIFA World Cup finals win for Africa when getting the better of Mexico.

Right: Mario Kempes celebrates scoring in the 1978 final. His two goals against the Netherlands took his tally to six in the tournament to earn the adidas Golden Shoe.

GROUP 1

Italy	2	France	1
Argentina	2	Hungary	1
Italy	3	Hungary	1
Argentina	2	France	1
France	3	Hungary	1
Italy	1	Argentina	0

	P	W	D	L	F	A	Pts
Italy	3	3	0	0	6	2	6
Argentina	3	2	0	1	6	3	4
France	3	1	0	2	5	5	2
Hungary	3	0	0	3	3	8	0

GROUP 2

Germany FR	0	Poland	0
Tunisia	3	Mexico	1
Poland	1	Tunisia	0
Germany FR	6	Mexico	0
Germany FR	0	Tunisia	0
Poland	3	Mexico	1

	P	W	D	L	F	A	Pts
Poland	3	2	1	0	4	1	5
Germany FR	3	1	2	0	6	0	4
Tunisia	3	1	1	1	3	2	3
Mexico	3	0	0	3	2	12	0

GROUP 3

Sweden	1	Brazil	1
Austria	2	Spain	1
Austria	1	Sweden	0
Brazil	0	Spain	0
Brazil	1	Austria	0
Spain	1	Sweden	0

	P	W	D	L	F	A	Pts
Austria	3	2	0	1	3	2	4
Brazil	3	1	2	0	2	1	4
Spain	3	1	1	1	2	2	3
Sweden	3	0	1	2	1	3	1

GROUP 4

Netherlands	3	Iran	0
Peru	3	Scotland	1
Scotland	1	Iran	1
Netherlands	0	Peru	0
Scotland	3	Netherlands	2
Peru	4	Iran	1

	P	W	D	L	F	A	Pts
Peru	3	2	1	0	7	2	5
Netherlands	3	1	1	1	5	3	3
Scotland	3	1	1	1	5	6	3
Iran	3	0	1	2	2	8	1

SECOND ROUND

GROUP A

Germany FR	0	Italy	0
Netherlands	5	Austria	1
Italy	1	Austria	0
Germany FR	2	Netherlands	2
Netherlands	2	Italy	1
Austria	3	Germany FR	2

	P	W	D	L	F	A	Pts
Netherlands	3	2	1	0	9	4	5
Italy	3	1	1	1	2	2	3
Germany FR	3	0	2	1	4	5	2
Austria	3	1	0	2	4	8	2

GROUP B

Brazil	3	Peru	0
Argentina	2	Poland	0
Poland	1	Peru	0
Argentina	0	Brazil	0
Brazil	3	Poland	1
Argentina	6	Peru	0

	P	W	D	L	F	A	Pts
Argentina	3	2	1	0	8	0	5
Brazil	3	2	1	0	6	1	5
Poland	3	1	0	2	2	5	2
Peru	3	0	0	3	0	10	0

THIRD-PLACE MATCH

Brazil	2	Italy	1

FINAL – 25 June: El Monumental, Buenos Aires

Argentina 3 Kempes (38, 105), Bertoni (115) **Netherlands** 1 Nanninga (82) After extra time HT: 1–0. Att: 71,483. Ref: Gonella (Italy)

Argentina: Fillol, Ardiles (Larrosa 65), Bertoni, Gallego, Galvan, Kempes, Luque, Olguin, Ortiz (Houseman 74), Passarella, Tarantini.

Netherlands: Jongbloed, Poortvliet, Krol, Jansen (Suurbier 72), Haan, R van de Kerkhof, W van de Kerkhof, Rensenbrink, Neeskens, Rep (Nanninga 59), Brandts.

Top scorer: 6 Kempes (Argentina)

1982 SPAIN

Shortly after returning from a two-year ban for match-fixing, Paolo Rossi fired in six goals, including a hat-trick against Brazil, as Italy ended a 44-year wait for their third FIFA World Cup triumph.

Rossi struck twice in the semi-finals against Poland and opened the scoring in a 3–1 final win over West Germany, who had booked their place in the decider by prevailing in the tournament's first penalty shoot-out, against France.

Norman Whiteside became the youngest ever player to feature in the finals, at 17 years and 41 days, and his Northern Ireland side secured a famous success when beating hosts Spain.

Above: Paolo Rossi (third left) opens the scoring in the final against West Germany, his sixth goal of the 1982 finals.

GROUP 1

Italy	0	Poland	0
Peru	0	Cameroon	0
Italy	1	Peru	1
Poland	0	Cameroon	0
Poland	5	Peru	1
Italy	1	Cameroon	1

	P	W	D	L	F	A	Pts
Poland	3	1	2	0	5	1	4
Italy	3	0	3	0	2	2	3
Cameroon	3	0	3	0	1	1	3
Peru	3	0	2	1	2	6	2

GROUP 3

Belgium	1	Argentina	0
Hungary	10	El Salvador	1
Argentina	4	Hungary	1
Belgium	1	El Salvador	0
Belgium	1	Hungary	1
Argentina	2	El Salvador	0

	P	W	D	L	F	A	Pts
Belgium	3	2	1	0	3	1	5
Argentina	3	2	0	1	6	2	4
Hungary	3	1	1	1	12	6	3
El Salvador	3	0	0	3	1	13	0

GROUP 5

Spain	1	Honduras	1
Yugoslavia	0	Northern Ireland	0
Spain	2	Yugoslavia	1
Honduras	1	Northern Ireland	1
Yugoslavia	1	Honduras	0
Northern Ireland	1	Spain	0

	P	W	D	L	F	A	Pts
N. Ireland	3	1	2	0	2	1	4
Spain	3	1	1	1	3	3	3
Yugoslavia	3	1	1	1	2	2	3
Honduras	3	0	2	1	2	3	2

GROUP 2

Algeria	2	Germany FR	1
Austria	1	Chile	0
Germany FR	4	Chile	1
Austria	2	Algeria	0
Algeria	3	Chile	2
Germany FR	1	Austria	0

	P	W	D	L	F	A	Pts
Germany FR	3	2	0	1	6	3	4
Austria	3	2	0	1	3	1	4
Algeria	3	2	0	1	5	5	4
Chile	3	0	0	3	3	8	0

GROUP 4

England	3	France	1
Czechoslovakia	1	Kuwait	1
England	2	Czechoslovakia	0
France	4	Kuwait	1
France	1	Czechoslovakia	1
England	1	Kuwait	0

	P	W	D	L	F	A	Pts
England	3	3	0	0	6	1	6
France	3	1	1	1	6	5	3
Czechoslovakia	3	0	2	1	2	4	2
Kuwait	3	0	1	2	2	6	1

GROUP 6

Brazil	2	Soviet Union	1
Scotland	5	New Zealand	2
Brazil	4	Scotland	1
Soviet Union	3	New Zealand	0
Soviet Union	2	Scotland	2
Brazil	4	New Zealand	0

	P	W	D	L	F	A	Pts
Brazil	3	3	0	0	10	2	6
Soviet Union	3	1	1	1	6	4	3
Scotland	3	1	1	1	8	8	3
New Zealand	3	0	0	3	2	12	0

SECOND ROUND

GROUP 1

Poland	3	Belgium	0
Soviet Union	1	Belgium	0
Poland	0	Soviet Union	0

	P	W	D	L	F	A	Pts
Poland	2	1	1	0	3	0	3
Soviet Union	2	1	1	0	1	0	3
Belgium	2	0	0	2	0	4	0

GROUP 2

Germany FR	0	England	0
Germany FR	2	Spain	1
Spain	0	England	0

	P	W	D	L	F	A	Pts
Germany FR	2	1	1	0	2	1	3
England	2	0	2	0	0	0	2
Spain	2	0	1	1	1	2	1

GROUP 3

Italy	2	Argentina	1
Brazil	3	Argentina	1
Italy	3	Brazil	2

	P	W	D	L	F	A	Pts
Italy	2	2	0	0	5	3	4
Brazil	2	1	0	1	5	4	2
Argentina	2	0	0	2	2	5	0

GROUP 4

France	1	Austria	0
Austria	2	Northern Ireland	2
France	4	Northern Ireland	1

	P	W	D	L	F	A	Pts
France	2	2	0	0	5	1	4
Austria	2	0	1	1	2	3	1
N. Ireland	2	0	1	1	3	6	1

SEMI-FINALS

Italy	2	Poland	0
Germany FR	3 (5)	France	3 (4)*

* After extra time (pens)

THIRD-PLACE MATCH

Poland	3	France	2

FINAL – 11 July: Santiago Bernabeu, Madrid

Italy 3 Rossi (57), Tardelli (69), Altobelli (81) **Germany FR 1** Breitner (83)
HT: 0–0. Att: 90,000. Ref: Coelho (Brazil).
Italy: Zoff, Bergomi, Cabrini, Collovati, Gentile, Scirea, Oriali, Tardelli, Conti, Graziani (Altobelli 7; Causio 89), Rossi.
Germany FR: Schumacher, Briegel, Breitner, Foerster, Dremmler (Hrubesch 62), Littbarski, Fischer, Rummenigge (Mueller 70), Stielike, Kaltz.
Top scorer: 6 Rossi (Italy)

1986 MEXICO

Argentina were crowned champions in a tournament dominated by the talent and trickery of their captain Diego Maradona, who was put on a pedestal alongside Pele following a series of superb displays.

He scored five times, including the controversial 'Hand of God' goal against England in the quarter-finals, but he also scored one of the greatest ever FIFA World Cup goals in the same match.

A hat-trick against Poland in their Group F match helped Gary Lineker win the adidas Golden Shoe as leading scorer, while Morocco became the first African side to survive the opening group stage by winning Group F.

The tournament also saw the Mexican wave introduced to the world.

Above: Diego Maradona holds the FIFA World Cup Trophy aloft after a tournament in which the Argentina captain was the star of the show.

GROUP A

Bulgaria	1	Italy	1
Argentina	3	Korea Republic	1
Italy	1	Argentina	1
Korea Republic	1	Bulgaria	1
Italy	3	Korea Republic	2
Argentina	2	Bulgaria	0

	P	W	D	L	F	A	Pts
Argentina	3	2	1	0	6	2	5
Italy	3	1	2	0	5	4	4
Bulgaria	3	0	2	1	2	4	2
Korea Rep	3	0	1	2	4	7	1

GROUP B

Mexico	2	Belgium	1
Paraguay	1	Iraq	0
Mexico	1	Paraguay	1
Belgium	2	Iraq	1
Mexico	1	Iraq	0
Paraguay	2	Belgium	2

	P	W	D	L	F	A	Pts
Mexico	3	2	1	0	4	2	5
Paraguay	3	1	2	0	4	3	4
Belgium	3	1	1	1	5	5	3
Iraq	3	0	0	3	1	4	0

GROUP C

France	1	Canada	0
Soviet Union	6	Hungary	0
France	1	Soviet Union	1
Hungary	2	Canada	0
France	3	Hungary	0
Soviet Union	2	Canada	0

	P	W	D	L	F	A	Pts
Soviet Union	3	2	1	0	9	1	5
France	3	2	1	0	5	1	5
Hungary	3	1	0	2	2	9	2
Canada	3	0	0	3	0	5	0

GROUP D

Brazil	1	Spain	0
Algeria	1	Northern Ireland	1
Brazil	1	Algeria	0
Spain	2	Northern Ireland	1
Brazil	3	Northern Ireland	0
Spain	3	Algeria	0

	P	W	D	L	F	A	Pts
Brazil	3	3	0	0	5	0	6
Spain	3	2	0	1	5	2	4
N Ireland	3	0	1	2	2	6	1
Algeria	3	0	1	2	1	5	1

GROUP E

Uruguay	1	Germany FR	1
Denmark	1	Scotland	0
Germany FR	2	Scotland	1
Denmark	6	Uruguay	1
Denmark	2	Germany FR	0
Scotland	0	Uruguay	0

	P	W	D	L	F	A	Pts
Denmark	3	3	0	0	9	1	6
Germany FR	3	1	1	1	3	4	3
Uruguay	3	0	2	1	2	7	2
Scotland	3	0	1	2	1	3	1

GROUP F

Morocco	0	Poland	0
Portugal	1	England	0
England	0	Morocco	0
Poland	1	Portugal	0
Portugal	1	Morocco	3
England	3	Poland	0

	P	W	D	L	F	A	Pts
Morocco	3	1	2	0	3	1	4
England	3	1	1	1	3	1	3
Poland	3	1	1	1	1	3	3
Portugal	3	1	0	2	2	4	2

ROUND OF 16

Mexico	2	Bulgaria	0	
Belgium	4	Soviet Union	3	*
Argentina	1	Uruguay	0	
Brazil	4	Poland	0	
France	2	Italy	0	
Germany FR	1	Morocco	0	
England	3	Paraguay	0	
Spain	5	Denmark	1	

* After extra time

QUARTER-FINALS

France	1 (4)	Brazil	1 (3)*
Germany FR	0 (4)	Mexico	0 (1)*
Belgium	1 (5)	Spain	1 (4)*
Argentina	2	England	1

* After extra time (pens)

SEMI-FINALS

Argentina	2	Belgium	0
Germany FR	2	France	0

THIRD-PLACE MATCH

France	4	Belgium	2	*

* After extra time

FINAL – 29 June: Estadio Azteca, Mexico City

Argentina 3 Brown (23), Valdano (56), Burruchaga (84) **Germany FR** 2 Rummenigge (74), Voeller (81)

HT: 1-0. Att: 114,600. Ref: Arppi Filho (Brazil)

Argentina: Pumpido, Batista, Brown, Burruchaga (Trobbiani 90), Cuciuffo, Maradona, Valdano, Enrique, Giusti, Olarticoechea, Ruggeri.

Germany FR: Schumacher, Briegel, Brehme, Foerster, Eder, Matthaeus, Magath (Hoeness 62), Rummenigge, Berthold, Jakobs, Allofs (Voeller 45).

Top scorer: 6 Lineker (England)

1990 ITALY

West Germany avenged their loss to Argentina four years earlier after Pedro Monzon became the first player to be sent off in a FIFA World Cup final before Andreas Brehme settled a tight affair from the penalty spot.

Franz Beckenbauer became only the second successful manager to have also lifted the trophy as a player as his side won the last tournament before German reunification.

Other notable memories include Italy striker Toto Schillaci emerging from relative obscurity to top the scoring charts, Cameroon forward Roger Milla dancing with delight after scoring and Paul Gascoigne crying during England's semi-final defeat.

Right: West Germany coach Franz Beckenbauer became only the second man to win the FIFA World Cup as both player and manager, following Mario Zagallo of Brazil, who won as a player in 1958 and 1962 and coach in 1970.

GROUP A

Italy	1	Austria	0
Czechoslovakia	5	USA	1
Italy	1	USA	0
Czechoslovakia	1	Austria	0
Italy	2	Czechoslovakia	0
Austria	2	USA	1

	P	W	D	L	F	A	Pts
Italy	3	3	0	0	4	0	6
Czechoslovakia	3	2	0	1	6	3	4
Austria	3	1	0	2	2	3	2
USA	3	0	0	3	2	8	0

GROUP B

Cameroon	1	Argentina	0
Romania	2	Soviet Union	0
Argentina	2	Soviet Union	0
Cameroon	2	Romania	1
Argentina	1	Romania	1
Soviet Union	4	Cameroon	0

	P	W	D	L	F	A	Pts
Cameroon	3	2	0	1	3	5	4
Romania	3	1	1	1	4	3	3
Argentina	3	1	1	1	3	2	3
Soviet Union	3	1	0	2	4	4	2

GROUP C

Brazil	2	Sweden	1
Costa Rica	1	Scotland	0
Brazil	1	Costa Rica	0
Scotland	2	Sweden	1
Brazil	1	Scotland	0
Costa Rica	2	Sweden	1

	P	W	D	L	F	A	Pts
Brazil	3	3	0	0	4	1	6
Costa Rica	3	2	0	1	3	2	4
Scotland	3	1	0	2	2	3	2
Sweden	3	0	0	3	3	6	0

GROUP D

Colombia	2	UAE	0
Germany FR	4	Yugoslavia	1
Yugoslavia	1	Colombia	0
Germany FR	5	UAE	1
Germany FR	1	Colombia	1
Yugoslavia	4	UAE	1

	P	W	D	L	F	A	Pts
Germany FR	3	2	1	0	10	3	5
Yugoslavia	3	2	0	1	6	5	4
Colombia	3	1	1	1	3	2	3
UAE	3	0	0	3	2	11	0

GROUP E

Belgium	2	Korea Republic	0
Uruguay	0	Spain	0
Belgium	3	Uruguay	1
Spain	3	Korea Republic	1
Spain	2	Belgium	1
Uruguay	1	Korea Republic	0

	P	W	D	L	F	A	Pts
Spain	3	2	1	0	5	2	5
Belgium	3	2	0	1	6	3	4
Uruguay	3	1	1	1	2	3	3
Korea Rep	3	0	0	3	1	6	0

GROUP F

England	1	Rep of Ireland	1
Netherlands	1	Egypt	1
England	0	Netherlands	0
Rep of Ireland	0	Egypt	0
England	1	Egypt	0
Rep of Ireland	1	Netherlands	1

	P	W	D	L	F	A	Pts
England	3	1	2	0	2	1	4
Rep of Ireland	3	0	3	0	2	2	3
Netherlands	3	0	3	0	2	2	3
Egypt	3	0	2	1	1	2	2

ROUND OF 16

Cameroon	2	Colombia	1	*
Czechoslovakia	4	Costa Rica	1	
Argentina	1	Brazil	0	
Germany FR	2	Netherlands	1	
Rep of Ireland	0 (5)	Romania	0 (4)*	
Italy	2	Uruguay	0	
Yugoslavia	2	Spain	1	*
England	1	Belgium	0	*

After extra time (pens)

QUARTER-FINALS

Argentina	0 (3)	Yugoslavia	0 (2) *
Italy	1	Rep of Ireland	0
Germany FR	1	Czechoslovakia	0
England	3	Cameroon	2 *

After extra time (pens)

SEMI-FINALS

Argentina	1 (4)	Italy	1 (3)*
Germany FR	1 (4)	England	1 (3)*

After extra time (pens)

THIRD-PLACE MATCH

Italy	2	England	1

FINAL – 8 July: Stadio Olimpico, Rome

Germany FR 1 Brehme (85 pen)   **Argentina** 0
HT: 0–0. Att: 73,603. Ref: Codesal Mendez (Mexico)
Germany FR: Illgner, Brehme, Kohler, Augenthaler, Buchwald, Littbarski, Haessler, Voeller, Matthaeus, Berthold (Reuter 73), Klinsmann.
Argentina: Goycochea, Basualdo, Burruchaga (Calderon 53), Dezotti, Maradona, Lorenzo, Sensini, Serrizuela, Ruggeri (Monzon 45), Simon, Troglio. **Sent off:** Monzon (65), Dezotti (87).
Top scorer: 6 Schillaci (Italy)

1994 USA

The USA put on a spectacular show watched by a record 3,587,538 fans, meaning the 52 matches attracted an average attendance of 69,000 spectators.

Plenty of goals were scored before the final failed to live up to expectations at the Rose Bowl in Pasadena, with Brazil eventually edging out Italy in the first decider to be settled by a penalty shootout after Roberto Baggio blazed his spot-kick over the crossbar.

Bulgaria were the surprise package, beating Germany on their way to the semi-finals, but the tournament was marred by defender Andres Escobar being murdered on his return home to Colombia after scoring an own goal in his side's loss to the hosts.

Right: Brazil players start their celebrations in Pasadena after Roberto Baggio's missed penalty gives them their fourth FIFA World Cup triumph in the first final to be decided by a penalty shootout.

GROUP A

USA	1	Switzerland	1
Romania	3	Colombia	1
Switzerland	4	Romania	1
USA	2	Colombia	1
Romania	1	USA	0
Colombia	2	Switzerland	0

	P	W	D	L	F	A	Pts
Romania	3	2	0	1	5	5	6
Switzerland	3	1	1	1	5	4	4
USA	3	1	1	1	3	3	4
Colombia	3	1	0	2	4	5	3

GROUP B

Cameroon	2	Sweden	2
Brazil	2	Russia	0
Brazil	3	Cameroon	0
Sweden	3	Russia	1
Russia	6	Cameroon	1
Brazil	1	Sweden	1

	P	W	D	L	F	A	Pts
Brazil	3	2	1	0	6	1	7
Sweden	3	1	2	0	6	4	5
Russia	3	1	0	2	7	6	3
Cameroon	3	0	1	2	3	11	1

GROUP C

Germany	1	Bolivia	0
Spain	2	Korea Republic	2
Germany	1	Spain	1
Korea Republic	0	Bolivia	0
Spain	3	Bolivia	1
Germany	3	Korea Republic	2

	P	W	D	L	F	A	Pts
Germany	3	2	1	0	5	3	7
Spain	3	1	2	0	6	4	5
Korea Rep	3	0	2	1	4	5	2
Bolivia	3	0	1	2	1	4	1

GROUP D

Argentina	4	Greece	0
Nigeria	3	Bulgaria	0
Argentina	2	Nigeria	1
Bulgaria	4	Greece	0
Nigeria	2	Greece	0
Bulgaria	2	Argentina	0

	P	W	D	L	F	A	Pts
Nigeria	3	2	0	1	6	2	6
Bulgaria	3	2	0	1	6	3	6
Argentina	3	2	0	1	6	3	6
Greece	3	0	0	3	0	10	0

GROUP E

Rep of Ireland	1	Italy	0
Norway	1	Mexico	0
Italy	1	Norway	0
Mexico	2	Rep of Ireland	1
Rep of Ireland	0	Norway	0
Italy	1	Mexico	1

	P	W	D	L	F	A	Pts
Mexico	3	1	1	1	3	3	4
Rep of Ireland	3	1	1	1	2	2	4
Italy	3	1	1	1	2	2	4
Norway	3	1	1	1	1	1	4

GROUP F

Belgium	1	Morocco	0
Netherlands	2	Saudi Arabia	1
Belgium	1	Netherlands	0
Saudi Arabia	2	Morocco	1
Netherlands	2	Morocco	1
Saudi Arabia	1	Belgium	0

	P	W	D	L	F	A	Pts
Netherlands	3	2	0	1	4	3	6
Saudi Arabia	3	2	0	1	4	3	6
Belgium	3	2	0	1	2	1	6
Morocco	3	0	0	3	2	5	0

ROUND OF 16

Germany	3	Belgium	2
Spain	3	Switzerland	0
Sweden	3	Saudi Arabia	1
Romania	3	Argentina	2
Netherlands	2	Rep of Ireland	0
Brazil	1	USA	0
Italy	2	Nigeria	1	*
Bulgaria	1 (3)	Mexico	1 (1)	*

* After extra time (pens)

QUARTER-FINALS

Italy	2	Spain	1
Brazil	3	Netherlands	2
Bulgaria	2	Germany	1
Sweden	2 (5)	Romania	2 (4)*

* After extra time (pens)

SEMI-FINALS

Italy	2	Bulgaria	1
Brazil	1	Sweden	0

THIRD-PLACE MATCH

Sweden	4	Bulgaria	0

FINAL – 17 July: Rose Bowl, Pasadena

Brazil 0 (3)   **Italy** 0 (2)   After extra time and penalties

HT: 0-0. **Att:** 94,194. **Ref:** Puhl (Hungary)

Brazil: Taffarel, Jorginho (Cafu 21), Mauro Silva, Branco, Bebeto, Dunga, Zinho (Viola 106), Romario, Aldair, Marcio Santos, Mazinho.

Italy: Pagliuca, Benarrivo, Maldini, Baresi, Mussi (Apolloni 34), R Baggio, Albertini, D Baggio (Evani 95), Berti, Donadoni, Massaro.

Top scorers: 6 Salenko (Russia), Stoichkov (Bulgaria)

1998 FRANCE

The FIFA World Cup finals featured 32 teams for the first time as qualifiers from Africa, Asia and the CONCACAF region increased and hosts France secured an inaugural success as the trophy stayed in the homeland of the tournament's father-figure Jules Rimet.

In the knockout rounds, Les Bleus beat Paraguay thanks to a golden goal, shaded Italy on penalties and saw off Croatia before a Zinedine Zidane double helped them crush Brazil 3-0 in the final.

Davor Suker of Croatia was the tournament's top scorer, while the game of the tournament saw England lose out to Argentina in a shootout despite a Michael Owen wonder goal as David Beckham was sent off.

GROUP A

Brazil	2	Scotland	1
Morocco	2	Norway	2
Scotland	1	Norway	1
Brazil	3	Morocco	0
Morocco	3	Scotland	0
Norway	2	Brazil	1

	P	W	D	L	F	A	Pts
Brazil	3	2	0	1	6	3	6
Norway	3	1	2	0	5	4	5
Morocco	3	1	1	1	5	5	4
Scotland	3	0	1	2	2	6	1

GROUP B

Cameroon	1	Austria	1
Italy	2	Chile	2
Chile	1	Austria	1
Italy	3	Cameroon	0
Italy	2	Austria	1
Chile	1	Cameroon	1

	P	W	D	L	F	A	Pts
Italy	3	2	1	0	7	3	7
Chile	3	0	3	0	4	4	3
Austria	3	0	2	1	3	4	2
Cameroon	3	0	2	1	2	5	2

GROUP C

Denmark	1	Saudi Arabia	0
France	3	South Africa	0
France	4	Saudi Arabia	0
South Africa	1	Denmark	1
France	2	Denmark	1
South Africa	2	Saudi Arabia	2

	P	W	D	L	F	A	Pts
France	3	3	0	0	9	1	9
Denmark	3	1	1	1	3	3	4
South Africa	3	0	2	1	3	6	2
Saudi Arabia	3	0	1	2	2	7	1

GROUP D

Paraguay	0	Bulgaria	0
Nigeria	3	Spain	2
Nigeria	1	Bulgaria	0
Spain	0	Paraguay	0
Spain	6	Bulgaria	1
Paraguay	3	Nigeria	1

	P	W	D	L	F	A	Pts
Nigeria	3	2	0	1	5	5	6
Paraguay	3	1	2	0	3	1	5
Spain	3	1	1	1	8	4	4
Bulgaria	3	0	1	2	1	7	1

GROUP E

Netherlands	0	Belgium	0
Mexico	3	Korea Republic	1
Netherlands	5	Korea Republic	0
Belgium	2	Mexico	2
Belgium	1	Korea Republic	1
Netherlands	2	Mexico	2

	P	W	D	L	F	A	Pts
Netherlands	3	1	2	0	7	2	5
Mexico	3	1	2	0	7	5	5
Belgium	3	0	3	0	3	3	3
Korea Rep	3	0	1	2	2	9	1

GROUP F

Yugoslavia	1	Iran	0
Germany	2	USA	0
Germany	2	Yugoslavia	2
Iran	2	USA	1
Germany	2	Iran	0
Yugoslavia	1	USA	0

	P	W	D	L	F	A	Pts
Germany	3	2	1	0	6	2	7
Yugoslavia	3	2	1	0	4	2	7
Iran	3	1	0	2	2	4	3
USA	3	0	0	3	1	5	0

GROUP G

Romania	1	Colombia	0
England	2	Tunisia	0
Colombia	1	Tunisia	0
Romania	2	England	1
Romania	1	Tunisia	1
England	2	Colombia	0

	P	W	D	L	F	A	Pts
Romania	3	2	1	0	4	2	7
England	3	2	0	1	5	2	6
Colombia	3	1	0	2	1	3	3
Tunisia	3	0	1	2	1	4	1

GROUP H

Croatia	3	Jamaica	1
Argentina	1	Japan	0
Croatia	1	Japan	0
Argentina	5	Jamaica	0
Jamaica	2	Japan	1
Argentina	1	Croatia	0

	P	W	D	L	F	A	Pts
Argentina	3	3	0	0	7	0	9
Croatia	3	2	0	1	4	2	6
Jamaica	3	1	0	2	3	9	3
Japan	3	0	0	3	1	4	0

ROUND OF 16

Brazil	4	Chile	1
Italy	1	Norway	0
Denmark	4	Nigeria	1
France	1	Paraguay	0 *
Germany	2	Mexico	1
Netherlands	2	Yugoslavia	1
Argentina	2 (4)	England	2 (3)*
Croatia	1	Romania	0

* After extra time (pens)

QUARTER-FINALS

France	0 (4)	Italy	0 (3) *
Brazil	3	Denmark	2
Croatia	3	Germany	0
Netherlands	2	Argentina	1

* After extra time (pens)

SEMI-FINALS

Brazil	1 (4)	Netherlands	1 (2)*
France	2	Croatia	1

* After extra time (pens)

THIRD-PLACE MATCH

Croatia	2	Netherlands	1

FINAL – 12 July: Stade de France, Paris

France 3   Zidane (27, 45), Petit (90)   **Brazil** 0

HT: 2-0. Att: 80,000. **Ref:** Belqola (Morocco)

France: Barthez, Lizarazu, Djorkaeff (Vieira 74), Deschamps, Desailly, Guivarc'h (Dugarry 66), Zidane, Thuram, Petit, Leboeuf, Karembeu (Boghossian 57). **Sent off:** Desailly 68.

Brazil: Taffarel, Cafu, Aldair, Junior Baiano, Cesar Sampaio (Edmundo 73), Roberto Carlos, Dunga, Ronaldo, Rivaldo, Leonardo (Denilson 46), Bebeto.

Top scorer: 6 Suker (Croatia)

Left: Ronaldo gets his hands on the FIFA World Cup Trophy after he scored both goals in the final, taking his tally to eight for the tournament, which earned him the adidas Golden Shoe.

2002 KOREA/JAPAN

Asia hosted the FIFA World Cup finals for the first time, with Brazil coming out on top for a record fifth time after adidas Golden Shoe winner Ronaldo scored both goals in a 2–0 defeat of Germany in the decider.

The tournament began with a number of shock results as Senegal beat holders France in the opening game on their way to the quarter-finals, while highly-rated Portugal and Argentina also failed to make it past the group stage.

The co-hosts both reached the knockout rounds, with Korea Republic getting as far as the last four by knocking out Italy and Spain, before losing to fellow surprise semi-finalists Turkey in the third-place play-off.

GROUP A

Senegal	1	France	0
Denmark	2	Uruguay	1
France	0	Uruguay	0
Denmark	1	Senegal	1
Denmark	2	France	0
Senegal	3	Uruguay	3

	P	W	D	L	F	A	Pts
Denmark	3	2	1	0	5	2	7
Senegal	3	1	2	0	5	4	5
Uruguay	3	0	2	1	4	5	2
France	3	0	1	2	0	3	1

GROUP B

Paraguay	2	South Africa	2
Spain	3	Slovenia	1
Spain	3	Paraguay	1
South Africa	1	Slovenia	0
Spain	3	South Africa	2
Paraguay	3	Slovenia	1

	P	W	D	L	F	A	Pts
Spain	3	3	0	0	9	4	9
Paraguay	3	1	1	1	6	6	4
South Africa	3	1	1	1	5	5	4
Slovenia	3	0	0	3	2	7	0

GROUP C

Brazil	2	Turkey	1
Costa Rica	2	China PR	0
Brazil	4	China PR	0
Costa Rica	1	Turkey	1
Brazil	5	Costa Rica	2
Turkey	3	China PR	0

	P	W	D	L	F	A	Pts
Brazil	3	3	0	0	11	3	9
Turkey	3	1	1	1	5	3	4
Costa Rica	3	1	1	1	5	6	4
China PR	3	0	0	3	0	9	0

GROUP D

Korea Republic	2	Poland	0
USA	3	Portugal	2
Korea Republic	1	USA	1
Portugal	4	Poland	0
Korea Republic	1	Portugal	0
Poland	3	USA	1

	P	W	D	L	F	A	Pts
Korea Rep	3	2	1	0	4	1	7
USA	3	1	1	1	5	6	4
Portugal	3	1	0	2	6	4	3
Poland	3	1	0	2	3	7	3

GROUP E

Rep of Ireland	1	Cameroon	1
Germany	8	Saudi Arabia	0
Germany	1	Rep of Ireland	1
Cameroon	1	Saudi Arabia	0
Germany	2	Cameroon	0
Rep of Ireland	3	Saudi Arabia	0

	P	W	D	L	F	A	Pts
Germany	3	2	1	0	11	1	7
Rep of Ireland	3	1	2	0	5	2	5
Cameroon	3	1	1	1	2	3	4
Saudi Arabia	3	0	0	3	0	12	0

GROUP F

England	1	Sweden	1
Argentina	1	Nigeria	0
Sweden	2	Nigeria	1
England	1	Argentina	0
Sweden	1	Argentina	1
Nigeria	0	England	0

	P	W	D	L	F	A	Pts
Sweden	3	1	2	0	4	3	5
England	3	1	2	0	2	1	5
Argentina	3	1	1	1	2	2	4
Nigeria	3	0	1	2	1	3	1

GROUP G

Mexico	1	Croatia	0
Italy	2	Ecuador	0
Croatia	2	Italy	1
Mexico	2	Ecuador	1
Mexico	1	Italy	1
Ecuador	1	Croatia	0

	P	W	D	L	F	A	Pts
Mexico	3	2	1	0	4	2	7
Italy	3	1	1	1	4	3	4
Croatia	3	1	0	2	2	3	3
Ecuador	3	1	0	2	2	4	3

GROUP H

Japan	2	Belgium	2
Russia	2	Tunisia	0
Japan	1	Russia	0
Tunisia	1	Belgium	1
Japan	2	Tunisia	0
Belgium	3	Russia	2

	P	W	D	L	F	A	Pts
Japan	3	2	1	0	5	2	7
Belgium	3	1	2	0	6	5	5
Russia	3	1	0	2	4	4	3
Tunisia	3	0	1	2	1	5	1

ROUND OF 16

Germany	1	Paraguay	0
England	3	Denmark	0
Senegal	2	Sweden	1 *
Spain	1 (3)	Rep of Ireland	1 (2)*
USA	2	Mexico	0
Brazil	2	Belgium	0
Turkey	1	Japan	0
Korea Republic	2	Italy	1 *

* After extra time (pens)

QUARTER-FINALS

Brazil	2	England	1
Germany	1	USA	0
Korea Rep	0 (5)	Spain	0 (3)*
Turkey	1	Senegal	0 *

* After extra time (pens)

SEMI-FINALS

Germany	1	Korea Rep	0
Brazil	1	Turkey	0

THIRD-PLACE MATCH

Turkey	3	Korea Republic	2

FINAL – 30 June: International Stadium, Yokohama

Brazil 2 Ronaldo (67, 79)   **Germany 0**
HT: 0–0. Att: 69,029. Ref: Collina (Italy)
Brazil: Marcos, Edmilson, Lucio, Roque Junior, Cafu, Kleberson, Gilberto Silva, Roberto Carlos, Ronaldinho (Juninho Paulista 85), Rivaldo, Ronaldo (Denilson 90).
Germany: Kahn, Linke, Ramelow, Metzelder, Frings, Schneider, Jeremies (Asamoah 77), Hamann, Bode (Ziege 84), Neuville, Klose (Bierhoff 74).
Top scorer: 8 Ronaldo (Brazil)

2006 GERMANY

Italy claimed their fourth triumph in dramatic fashion when beating France on penalties at Berlin's Olympic Stadium, having edged out hosts Germany in extra time in the semi-finals.

The Azzurri built their success around a superb defensive effort which saw them concede only twice in the whole tournament, with Gianluigi Buffon only beaten by an own goal and a Zinedine Zidane spot-kick prior to the concluding shootout. Zidane was awarded the adidas Golden Ball but the 33-year-old ended his amazing career on a low note when sent off in the decider, while Ronaldo scored a record 15th goal in FIFA World Cup finals.

GROUP A

Germany	4	Costa Rica	2
Ecuador	2	Poland	0
Germany	1	Poland	0
Ecuador	3	Costa Rica	0
Germany	3	Ecuador	0
Poland	2	Costa Rica	1

	P	W	D	L	F	A	Pts
Germany	3	3	0	0	8	2	9
Ecuador	3	2	0	1	5	3	6
Poland	3	1	0	2	2	4	3
Costa Rica	3	0	0	3	3	9	0

GROUP B

England	1	Paraguay	0
Trinidad & Tobago	0	Sweden	0
England	2	Trinidad & Tobago	0
Sweden	1	Paraguay	0
Sweden	2	England	2
Paraguay	2	Trinidad & Tobago	0

	P	W	D	L	F	A	Pts
England	3	2	1	0	5	2	7
Sweden	3	1	2	0	3	2	5
Paraguay	3	1	0	2	2	2	3
Trinidad & T	3	0	1	2	0	4	1

GROUP C

Argentina	2	Côte d'Ivoire	1
Netherlands	1	Serbia & Montenegro	0
Argentina	6	Serbia & Montenegro	0
Netherlands	2	Côte d'Ivoire	1
Netherlands	0	Argentina	0
Côte d'Ivoire	3	Serbia & Montenegro	2

	P	W	D	L	F	A	Pts
Argentina	3	2	1	0	8	1	7
Netherlands	3	2	1	0	3	1	7
Côte d'Ivoire	3	1	0	2	5	6	3
Serbia & M	3	0	0	3	2	10	0

GROUP D

Mexico	3	Iran	1
Portugal	1	Angola	0
Mexico	0	Angola	0
Portugal	2	Iran	0
Portugal	2	Mexico	1
Iran	1	Angola	1

	P	W	D	L	F	A	Pts
Portugal	3	3	0	0	5	1	9
Mexico	3	1	1	1	4	3	4
Angola	3	0	2	1	1	2	2
Iran	3	0	1	2	2	6	1

GROUP E

Italy	2	Ghana	0
Czech Republic	3	USA	0
Italy	1	USA	1
Ghana	2	Czech Republic	0
Italy	2	Czech Republic	0
Ghana	2	USA	1

	P	W	D	L	F	A	Pts
Italy	3	2	1	0	5	1	7
Ghana	3	2	0	1	4	3	6
Czech Rep	3	1	0	2	3	4	3
USA	3	0	1	2	2	6	1

GROUP F

Brazil	1	Croatia	0
Australia	3	Japan	1
Brazil	2	Australia	0
Japan	0	Croatia	0
Brazil	4	Japan	1
Croatia	2	Australia	2

	P	W	D	L	F	A	Pts
Brazil	3	3	0	0	7	1	9
Australia	3	1	1	1	5	5	4
Croatia	3	0	2	1	2	3	2
Japan	3	0	1	2	2	7	1

GROUP G

France	0	Switzerland	0
Korea Republic	2	Togo	1
France	1	Korea Republic	1
Switzerland	2	Togo	0
France	2	Togo	0
Switzerland	2	Korea Republic	0

	P	W	D	L	F	A	Pts
Switzerland	3	2	1	0	4	0	7
France	3	1	2	0	3	1	5
Korea Rep	3	1	1	1	3	4	4
Togo	3	0	0	3	1	6	0

GROUP H

Spain	4	Ukraine	0
Tunisia	2	Saudi Arabia	2
Spain	3	Tunisia	1
Ukraine	4	Saudi Arabia	0
Spain	1	Saudi Arabia	0
Ukraine	1	Tunisia	0

	P	W	D	L	F	A	Pts
Spain	3	3	0	0	8	1	9
Ukraine	3	2	0	1	5	4	6
Tunisia	3	0	1	2	3	6	1
Saudi Arabia	3	0	1	2	2	7	1

ROUND OF 16

Germany	2	Sweden	0	
Argentina	2	Mexico	1	*
England	1	Ecuador	0	
Portugal	1	Netherlands	0	
Italy	1	Australia	0	
Ukraine	0 (3)	Switzerland	0 (0)	*
Brazil	3	Ghana	0	
France	3	Spain	1	

* After extra time (pens)

QUARTER-FINALS

Germany	1 (4)	Argentina	1 (2)	*
Italy	3	Ukraine	0	
Portugal	0 (3)	England	0 (1)	*
France	1	Brazil	0	

* After extra time (pens)

SEMI-FINALS

| Italy | 2 | Germany | 0 | |
| France | 1 | Portugal | 0 | |

* After extra time

THIRD-PLACE MATCH

| Germany | 3 | Portugal | 1 |

FINAL – 9 July: Olympic Stadium, Berlin

Italy 1 (5)   Materazzi 19   **France** 1 (3)   Zidane (7, pen)   *After extra time and penalties*
HT: 1-1. Att: 69,000. Ref: Elizondo (Argentina).
Italy: Buffon, Grosso, Cannavaro, Gattuso, Toni, Totti (De Rossi 61), Camoranesi (Del Piero 86), Zambrotta, Perrotta (Iaquinta 61), Pirlo, Materazzi.
France: Barthez, Abidal, Vieira (Diarra 56), Gallas, Makelele, Malouda, Zidane, Henry (Wiltord 107), Thuram, Sagnol, Ribery (Trezeguet 100). **Sent off:** Zidane (110).
Top scorer: 5 Klose (Germany)

Left: Diego Forlan celebrates after scoring Uruguay's first goal during the FIFA World Cup semi-final against the Netherlands at the Green Point Stadium in Cape Town, a match the Dutch eventually won 3–2.

Right: Goalkeeper Iker Casillas holds up the FIFA World Cup Trophy after Spain had beaten the Netherlands after extra time in the 2010 final in South Africa.

2010 SOUTH AFRICA

Spain ended the country's long wait to be FIFA World Cup champions when they defeated the Netherlands 1–0 in the final at Soccer City thanks to a late goal by Andres Iniesta. The result ensured Spain became only the third country to be world and European champions at the same time.

South Africa did a great job of hosting the first FIFA World Cup to be held in Africa and the continent almost had a team in the semi-finals, only for Ghana to lose out on penalties to Uruguay.

The eventual champions lost 1–0 to Switzerland in their first game but then conceded only one goal in six matches and scored eight themselves. Germany looked strong, especially beating England 4–1 in the round of 16, but finished third place after losing to Spain in the semi-final. The hosts drew with Mexico and beat France, but missed out on the second stage on goal difference.

GROUP A

South Africa	1	Mexico	1
Uruguay	0	France	0
Uruguay	3	South Africa	0
Mexico	2	France	0
Uruguay	1	Mexico	0
South Africa	2	France	1

	P	W	D	L	F	A	Pts
Uruguay	3	2	1	0	4	0	7
Mexico	3	1	1	1	3	2	4
South Africa	3	1	1	1	3	5	4
France	3	0	1	2	1	4	1

GROUP B

Argentina	1	Nigeria	0
Korea Republic	2	Greece	0
Greece	2	Nigeria	1
Argentina	4	Korea Republic	1
Nigeria	2	Korea Republic	2
Argentina	2	Greece	0

	P	W	D	L	F	A	Pts
Argentina	3	3	0	0	7	1	9
Korea Rep	3	1	1	1	5	6	4
Greece	3	1	0	2	2	5	3
Nigeria	3	0	1	2	3	5	1

GROUP C

England	1	USA	1
Slovenia	1	Algeria	0
Slovenia	2	USA	2
England	0	Algeria	0
England	1	Slovenia	0
USA	1	Algeria	0

	P	W	D	L	F	A	Pts
USA	3	1	2	0	4	3	5
England	3	1	2	0	2	1	5
Slovenia	3	1	1	1	3	3	4
Algeria	3	0	1	2	0	2	1

GROUP D

Germany	4	Australia	0
Ghana	1	Serbia	0
Serbia	1	Germany	0
Ghana	1	Australia	1
Germany	1	Ghana	0
Australia	2	Serbia	1

	P	W	D	L	F	A	Pts
Germany	3	2	0	1	5	1	6
Ghana	3	1	1	1	2	2	4
Australia	3	1	1	1	3	6	4
Serbia	3	1	0	2	2	3	3

GROUP E

Netherlands	2	Denmark	0
Japan	1	Cameroon	0
Netherlands	1	Japan	0
Denmark	2	Cameroon	1
Japan	3	Denmark	1
Netherlands	2	Cameroon	1

	P	W	D	L	F	A	Pts
Netherlands	3	3	0	0	5	1	9
Japan	3	2	0	1	4	2	6
Denmark	3	1	0	2	3	6	3
Cameroon	3	0	0	3	2	5	0

GROUP F

Italy	1	Paraguay	1
New Zealand	1	Slovakia	1
Paraguay	2	Slovakia	0
Italy	1	New Zealand	1
Slovakia	3	Italy	2
Paraguay	0	New Zealand	0

	P	W	D	L	F	A	Pts
Paraguay	3	1	2	0	3	1	5
Slovakia	3	1	1	1	4	5	4
New Zealand	3	0	3	0	2	2	3
Italy	3	0	2	1	4	5	2

GROUP G

Côte d'Ivoire	0	Portugal	0
Brazil	2	Korea DPR	1
Brazil	3	Côte d'Ivoire	1
Portugal	7	Korea DPR	0
Portugal	0	Brazil	0
Côte d'Ivoire	3	Korea DPR	0

	P	W	D	L	F	A	Pts
Brazil	3	2	1	0	5	2	7
Portugal	3	1	2	0	7	0	5
Côte d'Ivoire	3	1	1	1	4	3	4
Korea DPR	3	0	0	3	1	12	0

GROUP H

Chile	1	Honduras	0
Switzerland	1	Spain	0
Chile	1	Switzerland	0
Spain	2	Honduras	0
Spain	2	Chile	1
Switzerland	0	Honduras	0

	P	W	D	L	F	A	Pts
Spain	3	2	0	1	4	2	6
Chile	3	2	0	1	3	2	6
Switzerland	3	1	1	1	1	1	4
Honduras	3	0	1	2	0	3	1

ROUND OF 16

Uruguay	2	Korea Rep	1
Ghana	2	USA	1	*
Germany	4	England	1
Argentina	3	Mexico	1
Holland	2	Slovakia	1
Brazil	3	Chile	0
Paraguay	0 (5)	Japan	0 (3)*
Spain	1	Portugal	0

* After extra time (pens)

QUARTER-FINALS

Holland	2	Brazil	1
Uruguay	1 (4)	Ghana	1 (2)*
Germany	4	Argentina	0
Spain	1	Paraguay	0

* After extra time (pens)

SEMI-FINALS

| Holland | 3 | Uruguay | 2 |
| Spain | 1 | Germany | 0 |

THIRD-PLACE MATCH

| Germany | 3 | Uruguay | 2 |

FINAL – 11 July: Soccer City Stadium, Johannesburg

Spain 1   Iniesta (116)   **Netherlands** 0   *After extra time*
HT: 0–0. Att: 84,490. Ref: Webb (England)
Spain: Casillas, Pique, Puyol, Iniesta, Villa (Torres 106), Xavi, Capdevila, Alonso (Fabregas 87), Ramos, Busquets, Pedro (Navas 60).
Netherlands: Stekelenburg, van der Wiel, Heitinga, Mathijsen, van Bronckhorst, van Bommel, Kuyt (Elia 71), de Jong (van der Vaart 99), van Persie, Robben. **Sent off:** Heitinga (109)
Top scorers: 5 Forlan (Uruguay), Mueller (Germany), Sneijder (Netherlands), Villa (Spain)

FIFA WORLD CUP™ RECORDS

Every FIFA World Cup finals has given players, teams and coaches the chance to clinch a place in the history books and those fortunate to be present in Brazil will be aiming to do the same. Whether they are breaking new ground with feats that have never been achieved before, or simply creating history with their presence in the tournament, there is no better time for a player to seize the moment with the world watching.

Germany's Lothar Matthaeus has played in five FIFA World Cups and has made more appearances in the finals than any other player.

FIFA WORLD CUP
Brasil

TEAM RECORDS

Some countries are regulars on the biggest footballing stage of all and eight have experienced the thrill of being crowned the best team in the world, while others have seized the chance to secure a place in the history books with special achievements.

● SAMBA STARS

Brazil hold the record for competing in the most FIFA World Cup tournaments to date, having participated in all 19 editions since the inaugural event kicked off in 1930. Italy and Germany are next, having each entered 17 editions, while South American nations Argentina and Mexico have competed in 15 and 14 respectively. Brazil have reached a total of seven finals – losing out in 1950 and 1998 – and have also won more matches than any other nation (67).

Above: Brazil's win over Germany at the 2002 FIFA World Cup was a record fifth success. This year's hosts are also the only country to have played in every edition and hold the record for most matches won.

● HOME HELP

Host nations have won the FIFA World Cup on six occasions down the years, the last time being in 1998 when France were crowned champions for the first time. Brazil can bank on passionate support in 2014 as they look to lift the trophy in front of their home fans for the first time in their history, having finished as runners-up in 1950 on the only other occasion when they were the hosts. Sweden also lost the final of 1958 in Solna having entertained the footballing world.

● NO FOREIGN AID

No country has ever won the FIFA World Cup under the guidance of a foreign manager, with the 18 winning coaches all leading their home nations to glory. In 19 editions of the tournament, only Vittorio Pozzo has won the trophy twice, having guided Italy to glory in 1934 and 1938. Brazil and Germany, meanwhile, are the only two countries to boast FIFA World Cup-winning players and managers. Mario Zagallo played for Brazil in 1958 and 1962 before leading his country to success in 1970 while Franz Beckenbauer captained Germany in 1974 and then triumphed from the dugout in 1990.

FIFA WORLD CUP™ WINNERS

Titles	Country	Years
5	Brazil	1958, 1962, 1970, 1994, 2002
4	Italy	1934, 1938, 1982, 2006
3	Germany	1954, 1974, 1990
2	Argentina	1978, 1986
2	Uruguay	1930, 1950
1	England	1966
1	France	1998
1	Spain	2010

● EUROPE EDGE AHEAD

The final of 1930 is not only remembered as being the showpiece of the maiden FIFA World Cup but it remains the only one which has not included at least one European team. Uruguay triumphed 4–2 over South American rivals Argentina in Montevideo to be crowned as the world's first champions but there have subsequently been eight all-European finals, including 2006 and 2010. The 1950 FIFA World Cup final was not held as a single game but as a four-way final round between Brazil, Uruguay, Spain and Sweden. Spain's success in 2010 means Europe has now edged ahead of South America 10–9 in FIFA World Cup wins but none of those successes came in South America.

Right: Laurent Blanc of France celebrates scoring the first ever golden-goal winner at a FIFA World Cup, against Paraguay in 1998.

● SWISS KEEP IT TIGHT

Switzerland set a unique record when they went out of the 2006 FIFA World Cup at the second-round stage – without conceding a single goal in all four of their matches. The Swiss held France to a goalless draw in their opening game before recording 2–0 wins over Togo and then Korea Republic to top their group. They subsequently met Ukraine in the knockout stages but bowed out on penalties following a 0–0 draw.

● FIRSTS FOR FRANCE

France boast a special relationship with the FIFA World Cup. The French played Mexico in the first ever match in 1930, during which Lucien Laurent claimed the honour of scoring the tournament's inaugural goal. Four years later, Les Bleus were involved in the first game to go to extra time when they played Austria, while their match against Germany in 1982 became the first to be settled by a penalty shootout. Finally, en route to their 1998 success on home soil, Laurent Blanc broke new ground when he became the first player to score a golden goal as his extra-time effort disposed of Paraguay.

● HUNGARY HIT 10

Hungary became the first and only team so far to score 10 goals in a match at the FIFA World Cup finals when they beat El Salvador 10–1 in 1982. The Hungarians had also previously scored nine goals when they beat Korea Republic 9–0 in 1954 and they share the record for the biggest margin of victory with Yugoslavia, who beat Zaire 9–0 in 1974. The record for the most goals in a FIFA World Cup game is 12, when Austria edged hosts Switzerland 7–5 in 1954.

Above: Spain's maiden win at the 2010 FIFA World Cup means European teams have won 10 of the 19 tournaments.

PLAYER RECORDS

Appearing at the FIFA World Cup finals is the pinnacle of a footballing career for most players and some have been fortunate enough to savour the experience on several occasions, while others have made an appearance very early or towards the end of their career.

● LONG SERVICE

Lothar Matthaeus may have made the most appearances but he has not enjoyed as much FIFA World Cup action as Paolo Maldini. The former Italy defender played two fewer games than Matthaeus but remained on the pitch for longer, playing 2,220 minutes compared to the German's 2,052. Matthaeus is one of only two players to have appeared at five FIFA World Cup tournaments, having appeared in each edition from 1982 to 1998. It is a record which he shares with Antonio Carbajal of Mexico, who made his bow in 1950 and was still part of the squad 16 years later.

Above: German midfielder Lothar Matthaeus has made more appearances at FIFA World Cups than any other player, and is one of only two men to appear in five tournaments.

Below: Norman Whiteside was only 17 years and 41 days old when he played in 1982.

MOST FIFA WORLD CUP™ APPEARANCES

Games	Player	Country
25	Lothar Matthaeus	Germany
23	Paolo Maldini	Italy
21	Diego Maradona	Argentina
	Uwe Seeler	Germany
	Wladyslaw Zmuda	Poland
20	Cafu	Brazil
	Grzegorz Lato	Poland
19	Berti Vogts	Germany
	Karl-Heinz Rummenigge	Germany
	Miroslav Klose	Germany
	Ronaldo	Brazil
	Wolfgang Overath	Germany

● BROTHERS AT ARMS

It was a proud moment for the Boateng family in 2010 when two brothers appeared on opposing teams for the first time at a FIFA World Cup. Jerome played for Germany and came up against half-brother Kevin-Prince, who was in midfield for Ghana. Both were born in Germany to a Ghanaian father but to different mothers and Kevin-Prince switched nationality just a month before the tournament.

● YOUNG GUN WHITESIDE

Northern Ireland forward Norman Whiteside is the youngest player to appear at the FIFA World Cup finals. He was aged only 17 years and 41 days when he was handed his international debut against Yugoslavia in 1982 – beating Pele's previous record set in 1958 – and he is one of seven players to have made a FIFA World Cup appearance before his 18th birthday. Pele holds the record for the youngest player to appear in the final, having featured in the 1958 showpiece aged 17 years and 249 days.

Player	Country	Years
Giovanni Ferrari	Italy	1934, 1938
Giuseppe Meazza	Italy	1934, 1938
Pele	Brazil	1958, 1970
Didi	Brazil	1958, 1962
Djalma Santos	Brazil	1958, 1962
Garrincha	Brazil	1958, 1962
Gilmar	Brazil	1958, 1962
Nilton Santos	Brazil	1958, 1962
Vava	Brazil	1958, 1962
Zagallo	Brazil	1958, 1962
Zito	Brazil	1958, 1962
Cafu	Brazil	1994, 2002

● GOLDEN OLDIES

Dino Zoff became both the oldest player and oldest captain to win the FIFA World Cup when he led Italy to glory in Spain in 1982, aged 40 years and 133 days. Zoff is one of five players to have appeared at the FIFA World Cup finals after his 40th birthday and four of them are goalkeepers. Fellow veteran shot-stoppers Pat Jennings of Northern Ireland, England's Peter Shilton and Tunisia keeper Ali Boumnijel have also achieved that feat, along with Cameroon forward Roger Milla.

● HARD TO BEAT

No goalkeeper has ever been harder to beat at the FIFA World Cup finals than Walter Zenga. The Italian went 517 minutes without conceding a goal when his country hosted the tournament in 1990, keeping three clean sheets during the group stage and then against Uruguay and Republic of Ireland during the knockout stage before finally conceding to Claudio Caniggia in the 67th minute of the semi-final against Argentina. He was unable to save any of Argentina's four spot-kicks, though, as Italy went out on penalties. Iker Casillas will have Zenga's record in his sights if he starts for Spain at the 2014 FIFA World Cup finals, having finished the 2010 tournament without conceding in 433 minutes.

● LEADING THE WAY

Three players have each captained their country in two FIFA World Cup finals but none have managed to lift the trophy on both occasions. Karl-Heinz Rummenigge was the German captain for the defeats in the 1982 and 1986 finals, and Diego Maradona could not repeat Argentina's 1986 triumph four years later in Italy. Similarly, Dunga of Brazil was the winning captain in 1994 but was then on the losing side in 1998. Maradona holds the record for the most appearances as captain at the FIFA World Cup finals with 16 between 1986 and 1994.

Above: Brazil full-back Cafu is the 12th and most recent player to have won two FIFA World Cup finals.

Left: Italy goalkeeper Walter Zenga went a record 517 minutes without conceding a goal at the 1990 FIFA World Cup.

● MAKING A CHANGE

Anatoli Puzach of the Soviet Union made history when he became the first substitute in the history of the FIFA World Cup finals. The 1970 tournament in Mexico was the first at which substitutions were allowed, with both teams permitted two changes, and Puzach replaced Viktor Serebrianikov at half-time during the goalless draw with the hosts. FIFA increased the number of substitutions allowed to three at the 1998 finals.

GOALSCORING RECORDS

The old adage in football is that "goals win matches" and most fans come to watch goals being scored. Most FIFA World Cup record-breaking goalscorers become legends overnight, but others enjoy just one day in the sun.

● KLOSE TO SECOND

Germany's Miroslav Klose does not have the panache of Gerd Mueller, the silky midfield skills of Michael Ballack and Lothar Matthaeus, or the defensive genius of Franz Beckenbauer. He does, however, love records and he sits second in all-time goals for Germany (67) and second in appearances (127). When it comes to FIFA World Cup finals, guess what? Klose is second, too. He shares that mark – 14 goals – with Mueller, who netted his in just two tournaments, compared to three for Polish-born Klose. When he claimed the 2006 FIFA World Cup Golden Shoe, he became Germany's first winner since Mueller in 1970.

Above: Germany striker Miroslav Klose scores the opening goal against Ecuador at the 2006 FIFA World Cup. He won the tournament's Golden Shoe with five goals.

● THREE IS UNIQUE

Geoff Hurst of England is the only man to have scored a hat-trick in the FIFA World Cup final. In 1966, Hurst was second choice at the start of the tournament and only got his place when Jimmy Greaves was injured. He scored in the quarter-final victory over Argentina and kept his place for the semi-final against Portugal and the final against West Germany. Hurst cancelled out Helmut Haller's opening goal in the first half, scored the most controversial FIFA World Cup final goal in extra time to make it 3–2 and then, with seconds remaining, completed a perfect hat-trick (header, right-foot shot and left-foot shot).

● GOAL A GAME JUST ISN'T ENOUGH FOR FONTAINE

France's Just Fontaine set a record at the 1958 FIFA World Cup that may never be beaten. He scored 13 times in the tournament, starting with a hat-trick in the 7–3 defeat of Paraguay, twice in a 3–2 win over Yugoslavia and once when Scotland were beaten 2–1. Northern Ireland were brushed aside 4–0 by the rampant Frenchmen in the quarter-final, Fontaine netting twice, but France lost in the semi-final, when Pele inspired Brazil to a 5–2 win, despite another Fontaine goal. In the third-place match, he excelled against West Germany, scoring four times in a 6–3 win.

FIFA WORLD CUP™ LEADING GOALSCORERS BY TOURNAMENT

Year	Host	Player (Country)	Total
1930	Uruguay	Guillermo Stabile (Argentina)	8
1934	Italy	Oldrich Nejedly (Czechoslovakia)	5
1938	France	Leonidas (Brazil)	7
1950	Brazil	Ademir (Brazil)	9
1954	Switzerland	Sandor Kocsis (Hungary)	11
1958	Sweden	Just Fontaine (France)	13
1962	Chile	Garrincha (Brazil), Vava (Brazil)	4
		Leonel Sanchez (Chile)	4
		Drazan Jerkovic (Yugoslavia)	4
		Florian Albert (Hungary)	4
		Valentin Ivanov (Soviet Union)	4
1966	England	Eusebio (Portugal)	9
1970	Mexico	Gerd Mueller (West Germany)	10
1974	West Germany	Grzegorz Lato (Poland)	7
1978	Argentina	Mario Kempes (Argentina)	6
1982	Spain	Paolo Rossi (Italy)	6
1986	Mexico	Gary Lineker (England)	6
1990	Italy	Salvatore Schillaci (Italy)	6
1994	United States	Oleg Salenko (Russia)	6
		Hristo Stoichkov (Bulgaria)	6
1998	France	Davor Suker (Croatia)	6
2002	Korea/Japan	Ronaldo (Brazil)	8
2006	Germany	Miroslav Klose (Germany)	5
2010	South Africa	Diego Forlan (Uruguay)	5
		Thomas Mueller (Germany)	5
		Wesley Sneijder (Netherlands)	5
		David Villa (Spain)	5

No.	Player	Country	Years
15	Ronaldo	Brazil	1998, 2002, 2006, 2010
14	Gerd Mueller	West Germany	1970, 1974
	Miroslav Klose	Germany	2002, 2006, 2010
13	Just Fontaine	France	1958
12	Pele	Brazil	1958, 1962, 1966, 1970
11	Sandor Kocsis	Hungary	1954
	Jurgen Klinsmann	West Germany	1990, 1994, 1998
10	Helmut Rahn	West Germany	1954, 1958
	Teofilo Cubillas	Cuba	1970, 1978, 1982
	Grzegorz Lato	Poland	1974, 1978, 1982
	Gary Lineker	England	1986, 1990
	Gabriel Batistuta	Argentina	1994, 1998, 2002

Above: Roger Milla celebrates a goal against Colombia at the 1990 FIFA World Cup. He became the oldest goalscorer when, aged 42, he netted against Russia in 1994.

● THE MILLA'S TALE

Roger Milla made his debut at the Spain 1982 FIFA World Cup, aged 30, when Cameroon scored once in three draws and were eliminated. However, Milla was a star at the 1990 FIFA World Cup, helping his country to the quarter-finals, where they lost 3–2 to England. His exotic goal celebration was first seen in a 2–1 defeat of Romania, but more famously when he scored twice to beat Colombia in the second round. Four years later, he made his final appearance, against Russia on 28 June, when at 42 years and 39 days, he became the FIFA World Cup finals' oldest goalscorer.

● RONALDO ON HIS OWN

Brazil's Ronaldo holds the FIFA World Cup finals record with 15 goals, scored across four tournaments. He was at his peak in the 2002 FIFA World Cup, when he scored eight times, including both goals in the 2–0 final victory over Germany. Four years earlier, Ronaldo had been Brazil's best player as they reached the final against hosts France. But Ronaldo suffered some type of medical emergency on the eve of the final. Originally omitted from the team-sheet, he was hurriedly re-instated but was not the force he had been in previous matches as Brazil slumped to a 3–0 defeat.

● JAIRZINHO'S TOUR DE FORCE

The Brazil team which won the 1970 FIFA World Cup is considered by many to be the greatest ever, with stars such as Carlos Alberto, Gerson, Tostao, Rivelino and, of course, the legendary Pele. But their most consistent scorer was Jairzinho, who became the first man to net in every match, including the final. He scored seven goals in six matches, getting two in Brazil's opening 4–1 victory over Czechoslovakia. His most crucial goal was the only one of the game against England and he was the third Brazilian on the scoresheet in the 4–1 victory over Italy in the final.

● FIVE-STAR SALENKO CRUSHES CAMEROON

When Russia played Cameroon at Stanford Stadium, San Francisco, on 28 June, both teams were saying goodbye to the 1994 FIFA World Cup at the group stage. Russia, however, made their exit memorable. Oleg Salenko grabbed a first-half hat-trick, scoring after 15, 41 and 44 minutes. Roger Milla pulled a goal back a minute after half-time, but Salenko was not finished. He became the first man ever to score five times in one FIFA World Cup finals match with further goals after 72 and 75 minutes. The agony was not over for Cameroon as Dmitri Radchenko made it 6–1.

Right: Ronaldo celebrates scoring Brazil's first goal of the 2002 FIFA World Cup final. He won the adidas Golden Shoe with eight goals and, with 15, is the all-time leading scorer.

MORE RECORDS

Which teams have the most success from the penalty spot? And should you go first or second in a shootout? The answers and more FIFA World Cup trivia are here as we examine other interesting facts and statistics.

Left: Spain's Iker Casillas denies Paraguay forward Oscar Cardozo, one of two penalties he saved at the 2002 FIFA World Cup.

● CASILLAS IS SPOT ON

Goalkeeper Iker Casillas has played a vital role for Spain in the FIFA World Cup. The Real Madrid man became the third goalkeeper to captain the winning team in a final as Spain beat the Netherlands in 2010, emulating Italians Gianpiero Combi and Dino Zoff. Casillas is also the only shot-stopper to save a penalty in normal time at two different tournaments. He kept out Ian Harte's effort for the Republic of Ireland during a second-round match in 2002 and denied Paraguay forward Oscar Cardozo in the 2010 quarter-finals.

● A GAME FOR ALL AGES

Otto Rehhagel made history in South Africa four years ago when he became the oldest coach in the history of the FIFA World Cup finals. The German was 71 years and 317 days old when his Greece team were eliminated after a 2-0 defeat to Argentina. At the other end of the spectrum, Juan Jose Tramutola remains the youngest ever coach at the finals, having been in charge of Argentina in 1930 aged only 27 years and 267 days.

● FIRST UP IS BEST

Team captains and coaches in Brazil may be interested to know that the team taking the first spot-kick has gone on to win the last seven penalty shootouts at the FIFA World Cup. The last time a team went second and won a shootout was back in 2002 when Spain beat the Republic of Ireland.

FIFA WORLD CUP™ FINALS ATTENDANCES

Year	Country	Total	Average
1930	Uruguay	434,500	24,139
1934	Italy	358,000	21,059
1938	France	376,000	20,889
1950	Brazil	1,043,500	47,432
1954	Switzerland	889,500	34,212
1958	Sweden	919,580	26,274
1962	Chile	899,074	28,096
1966	England	1,635,000	51,094
1970	Mexico	1,603,975	50,124
1974	Germany	1,768,152	46,530
1978	Argentina	1,546,151	40,688
1982	Spain	2,109,723	40,572
1986	Mexico	2,393,331	46,026
1990	Italy	2,516,348	48,391
1994	USA	3,587,538	68,991
1998	France	2,785,100	43,517
2002	Korea/Japan	2,705,197	42,269
2006	Germany	3,359,439	52,491
2010	South Africa	3,178,856	46,670
Total		34,108,964	44,182

FIFA WORLD CUP™ PENALTY SHOOTOUTS

Country	Won	Lost
Germany/W Germany	4	0
Argentina	3	1
Brazil	2	1
France	2	2
Belgium	1	0
Bulgaria	1	0
Paraguay	1	0
Portugal	1	0
Korea Republic	1	0
Sweden	1	0
Ukraine	1	0
Uruguay	1	0
Yugoslavia	1	0
Republic of Ireland	1	1
Spain	1	2
Italy	1	3
Ghana	0	1
Netherlands	0	1
Japan	0	1
Switzerland	0	1
Mexico	0	2
Romania	0	2
England	0	3

● BAD BOYS

Argentina have the worst disciplinary record in FIFA World Cup finals history, having collected 103 yellow cards and 10 red across 70 matches between 1930 and 2010. Brazil have had most players sent off, with Felipe Melo's red card during their 2010 quarter-final defeat by the Netherlands the 11th in their history. Germany/West Germany have been shown 104 yellow and seven red in 99 games, while Italy have racked up 87 bookings and seven red cards in 80 encounters. Spain have an impressive disciplinary record of only one dismissal in 56 matches.

● FAMILIAR FACE

No coach has been to more FIFA World Cup finals than Brazilian Carlos Alberto Parreira, who has been in charge at six tournaments. The highlight of his coaching career came in 1994 when he guided his native country to glory in the USA. He was also in charge of Brazil at the FIFA World Cup 2006, and was coach of hosts South Africa four years ago. His other appointments were as coach of Kuwait (1982), the United Arab Emirates (1990) and Saudi Arabia (1998).

Right: Carlos Alberto Parreira has managed five different nations at six separate FIFA World Cups, including his native country, Brazil, twice.

● UNLUCKY RED

Red is seen as a lucky colour in some parts of the world but a team wearing red has not won the FIFA World Cup since England in 1966. Spain could have ended that streak four years ago but had to wear their dark blue change kit in the final against the Netherlands, although they changed into their usual red shirts before receiving the trophy from FIFA president Joseph S. Blatter. Spain's success in 2010 was also the first time since 1966 that a team wearing their second kit had won the final.

Above: No team since England in 1966 has won a FIFA World Cup final wearing red.

● THE LONGEST WAIT

Italy hold the record for the longest wait to regain the FIFA World Cup. Having won back-to-back tournaments in 1934 and 1938, the Azzurri had to wait 44 years before their next title came around in 1982. Current champions Spain had the longest wait between a top-four finish. Before their triumph in 2010, they had not finished as high since their fourth place in the final group in Brazil in 1950.

FIFA WORLD CUP
Brasil

Left: The adidas brazuca, the official match ball for the 2014 FIFA World Cup Brazil.

PRESS ASSOCIATION SPORT

Editor	Andrew McDermott.
Contributors	Colin Armitage, Liam Blackburn, James Cann, Andrew Carless, James Crawley, Callum Dent, Pete Evans, Tony Kelshaw, Frank Malley, James O'Brien, Euan Parsons, Glen Robertson, Matt Somerford, Jonathan Veal, Mark Walker, Drew Williams, Martyn Ziegler.
Design	Mark Tattersall.

PICTURES

AAP, ABACA Press France, Alpha, Associated Press, Atlantico, Belga Belgium, Chelsea FC, Demotix, DPA Germany, EFE Spain, Empics, Gabriel Piko, Landov, Press Association Images, Pixsell, Sports Inc – Back Page Pix, TT News Agency, VI Images.